More Effective Agile

A Roadmap for Software Leaders

Reviewer Guidelines

Thank you for your interest in reviewing this pre-publication copy of *More Effective Agile: A Roadmap for Software Leaders*.

This book is largely informed by experiences my company has had working with organizations in their Agile adoptions. I hope you will be willing to enrich the book by sharing your experiences.

I have found on other books that some review practices are particularly beneficial. I have listed a few guidelines here that are designed to maximize the value of the time you spend on your review.

How To Send Me Comments

The easiest way to send me comments is by email (stevemcc@construx.com). It will be a tremendous help to me if you can title your email "MEA Review". That titling convention helps get email past my spam filter (I'd hate to lose your review comments in my spam folder) and also helps me organize the hundreds of review emails I receive.

For specific comments, I'd appreciate it if you would identify the line number and then make your comment. Here are some examples:

> *64. You misspelled "your"*
>
> *436. Didn't Deming refer to this as PDSA in his later years?*

Line numbers are unique across the manuscript, so this convention makes it easy for you to identify where you are in the manuscript with a minimal amount of effort.

I prefer this approach to making comments directly in the pdf, which ends up being ambiguous more often than you might think!

Kinds of Comments

I am looking for comments of all kinds, but I am most interested in substantive, content-oriented comments. If you're interested enough in this book's topic to read a draft, I'm interested in seeing your comments.

If you think the writing style doesn't work for the leadership audience or you find places where the writing is unclear or misses the point, I am definitely interested in receiving those comments.

Does each chapter discuss everything it should? Is anything essential overlooked?

Does the chapter go into too much detail anywhere? Is there anything that's going to confuse your boss or team if you give them a copy of the book?

Are there sections you just couldn't get through because they were too boring? (Please tell me which ones!)

If you think the book's organization could be improved, please tell me. Does it need another chapter? Should one of the chapters be removed? Should one chapter be split into two chapters, or two chapters combined into one? I'd like it most if you could tell me how you think the organization could be improved, but just telling me that something just doesn't seem quite right can also be useful.

Sometimes people think that only critical comments are useful, but I have found that both positive and negative comments are useful. Sometimes a section will be a little controversial. If I get only the negative comments, I might feel like chucking it. If I also receive positive comments, then I might keep it, or I might acknowledge in the book that people feel strongly about the topic and do a better job of presenting multiple sides of the issue.

Why Should You Review This Book?

I can't tell you why you should review this book, but I'll tell you why I review other people's books:

It's easier for me to concentrate on and comprehend a book I'm reviewing than a book I am just reading for general knowledge's sake.

I like having a chance to influence the contents of books that will be used by the software industry. I like having a chance to correct misstatements and put in my 2 cents before the book is printed.

I enjoy seeing my name listed in the Acknowledgments.

I think part of the responsibility of someone who cares about the profession is to try to improve the profession. That can be done by reviewing someone's manuscript (as well as other ways, of course).

I only review books I want to read, so most of the time I spend reviewing a book is time I would have spent reading it anyway.

Acknowledging Your Input

If I use your comments, I'll gladly acknowledge your input on MEA's Acknowledgments page. Depending on the volume of comments I receive, I may not be able to acknowledge every email that comes in, especially if the comment is one that I've received several times already.

Send me email about MEA at stevemcc@construx.com.

Thank you for your interest in the book! I look forward to your comments!

More Effective Agile

More Effective Agile

A Roadmap for Software Leaders

Steve McConnell

Published by

Construx Press
10900 NE 8th Street, Suite 1350
Bellevue, WA 98004
www.construx.com

Library of Congress Cataloging-in-Publication Data

McConnell, Steven C.

More Effective Agile: A Roadmap for Software Leaders / Steve McConnell. —1st ed.

p. cm.

Includes bibliographical references and index.

ISBN 978-1-7335182-0-8 paperback 978-1-7335182-1-5

1. Computer software—development. 2. Agile development. I. Title.

QA76.76.D47M39 2019 [tbd]
005.1 –dc22 [tbd]

First Edition

1 2 3 4 5 6 7 8 9 10

Printed in the United States of America

Contents

MORE EFFECTIVE AGILE ORGANIZATIONS

CLOSING

Detailed Contents

INTRODUCTION TO MORE EFFECTIVE AGILE

More Effective Agile

Introduction to More Effective Agile

CHAPTER ONE

Introduction

My company was working with a digital content firm that had both onshore and offshore development staffs. About 70% of the staff was offshore. The company leaders were not sure how well their multi-site strategy was working.

Through a disciplined Scrum implementation that included rigorous productivity measurement and candid retrospectives, the numbers made clear that the overhead of working with the offshore staff was higher than the offshore staff's total output. The company eliminated the offshore staff, and the elimination of that overhead caused a doubling of overall output, despite eliminating 70% of the staff— actually, *because of* eliminating that staff, combined with other process improvements. The changes saved millions of dollars in development costs, and those savings will continue into the foreseeable future.

Unfortunately, these results are nowhere close to average because most implementations of Agile practices are not effective. Figure 1-1 shows the average Scrum project my company has seen compared to a healthy Scrum project.[1]

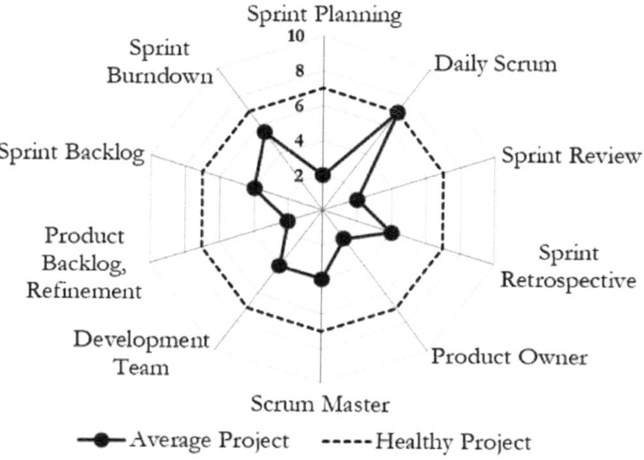

Figure 1-1

Average Scrum project compared to a healthy Scrum project.

In this figure, a score of 7 indicates a practice is being used effectively and a score below 5 indicates the practice is used sporadically. (Scoring is described in more detail in Chapter 5). We typically see only one of Scrum's key practices being used effectively (daily Scrum)—the rest of Scrum's practices are used sporadically or not at all.

---

[1] Scrum is not the only Agile practice, but if a company is not using Scrum well, it is probably not using other Agile practices well either. The effectiveness of an organization's Scrum implementation provides a useful window into the organization's use of Agile practices overall.

The average organization cannot achieve results similar to the digital content firm's results because its adoption of Agile practices is not effective. Markedly better performance is possible.

Why Effective Agile Matters to Your Business

Every company wants more effective software development for its own sake. They also want more effective software development because software enables so many other business functions. The *State of DevOps Report* reported that, "Firms with high-performing IT organizations were twice as likely to exceed their profitability, market share and productivity goals" (Puppet Labs, 2014). High-performing companies were twice as likely to meet or exceed their goals for customer satisfaction, quality and quantity of work, operating efficiency, and other organizational objectives.

Doesn't every software leader want that?

Of course they do, and selective, well-informed use of modern Agile practices offers a proven path toward more effective software development and all the benefits that go with it.

Agile Yesterday and Today

In the early 2000s, there were significant questions about Agile's ability to support quality, predictability, large projects, measured process improvement, and work in regulated industries. At the time, those were valid concerns. Today, the use of modern Agile practices offers the opportunity to improve quality, predictability, productivity, and throughput all at the same time.

Much of the Agile literature has focused on high-flying, high-growth companies in new markets, such as Netflix, Amazon, Etsy, Spotify, and other similar companies. But what if you're company makes software that's less leading edge? What if you don't release to customers 100 times per day? What about all the companies that make software for scientific instruments, office machines, medical devices, consumer electronics, heavy machinery, or process control equipment? What if you're working on internal systems for employee benefits, inventory management, shipping, CRM, or research?

For the past 15 years, my company, Construx Software, has worked both with leading-edge and traditional organizations to double, triple, and even quadruple measured productivity in short periods of time using Agile practices.

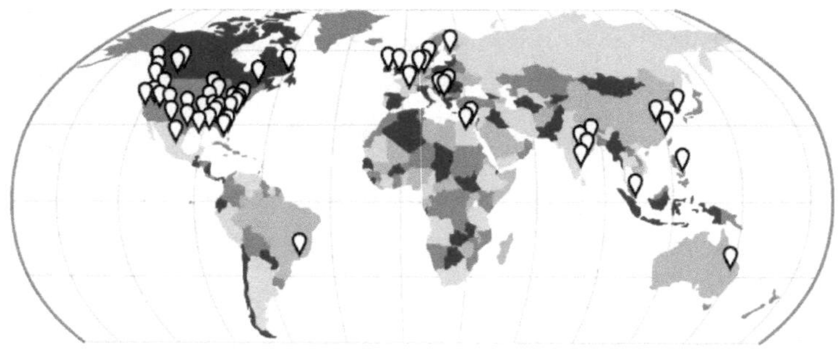

Figure 1-2

Countries, states, and provinces where Construx Software has helped with Scrum implementations and Agile adoptions.

These practices work for virtually all kinds of software. In addition to high-profile internet and mobile applications, they work for embedded software, combined hardware/software systems, scientific devices, process control systems, healthcare products, games, entertainment platforms, research projects, government initiatives—and many other kinds of software.

If you work in one of these less-than-high-flying industries, there's more good news: companies have been using Agile practices long enough that it's now possible to learn from their experience without needing to struggle through the school of hard knocks yourself.

Why Some Agile Adoptions Disappoint

Despite all these lessons learned, most organizations struggle with their Agile adoptions.

One reason is that the history of Agile software development has been an archetypal example of the Gartner Hype Cycle, shown in Figure 1-2. The initial promises were inflated, many early Agile adoptions were disappointing, achieving results took longer than planned, and the software industry has needed time and experience to differentiate the ineffective missteps from the genuine advances.

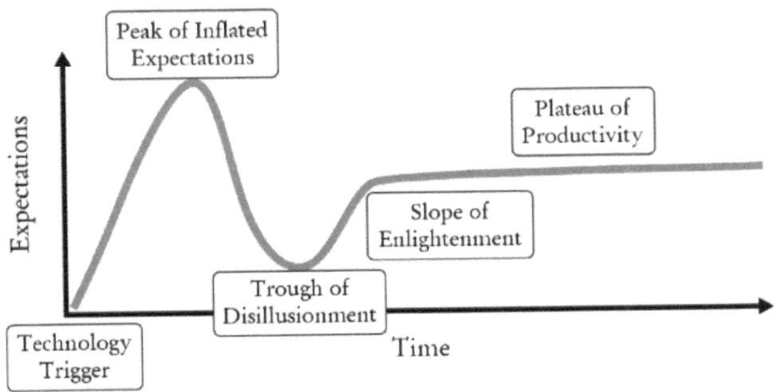

Figure 1-3
The Gartner Hype Cycle shows that each new technology or innovation experiences a predictable pattern of fluctuating expectations before stabilizing at the "Plateau of Productivity."

A related reason is that the term "Agile" has become an umbrella term that covers myriad practices, principles, and theories—some of which work well, and some of which do not. Some Agile adoptions fail due to selection of ineffective practices.

Even for practices that ultimately work, organizations still fall prey to dynamics related the Innovation Adoption J-Curve, shown in Figure 1-3. According to the J-Curve, an organization goes through a learning curve while it adopts an innovation. That learning curve implies a temporary period of effectiveness that's lower than before the change. In essence, the organization needs to learn to walk again before it learns to run faster.

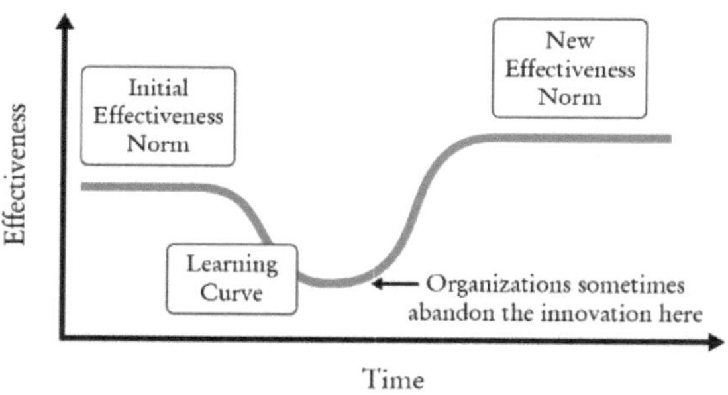

Figure 1-4

The Innovation Adoption J-Curve. Innovations typically require a period of learning investment during which effectiveness decreases temporarily before it increases again and re-establishes at a higher level.

While the organization is moving through the J-Curve, there's a destructive interaction between the J-Curve and the Hype Cycle. The "Learning Curve" portion of the J-Curve coincides with the "Trough of Disillusionment" phase in the Hype cycle. An organization sees its effectiveness declining, and sometimes it abandons its new Agile practice before it is able to work through the learning curve and reach a new, higher level of effectiveness.

Who This Book Is For

This book is for executives, VPs, Directors, managers, and other leaders of software organizations who want to ensure an effective Agile adoption in your organization. If you have a technical background but are not very deep in modern Agile practices, this book is for you. If you have a *nontechnical* background, this book is also for you. If you learned a lot about Agile practices 10–15 years ago but haven't updated your knowledge of modern Agile since then, this book is for you. And, most important, if your organization has adopted Agile development and you are not satisfied with the results, this book is for you.

This book is not intended as a guide for Agile pundits or consultants. It does not focus on leading-edge practices that seem promising today but are not yet proven. The history of Agile development is rich with practices that one or two enthusiasts used successfully in a handful of organizations but that ultimately were not found to be generally useful. This book does not dwell on those limited-use practices.

How This Book is Different From Other Agile Books

Most books about Agile development are written by advocates. They're advocating a specific Agile practice, or they're promoting Agile overall.

I am not an Agile advocate, per se. I'm an advocate for "things that work" and I'm an opponent of "things that over-promise with no evidence."

I could not have written this book 15 years ago because the software world had not accumulated enough on-the-ground experience with Agile development to know with any confidence what was working and what wasn't.

Today, the situation is different. The software industry has gained significant experience with Agile. We have learned that some of the practices that were the most publicized 15 years ago are not very effective, while other practices that were less publicized 15 years ago have emerged as the highly reliable workhorses of effective modern Agile implementations.

This book addresses the topics that businesses care about but that Agile pundits often neglect: common challenges with Agile implementations, how to implement Agile in only part of your organization, Agile's support for predictability, the best ways to use Agile on geographically distributed teams, and using Agile in regulated industries, just to name a few of the practical topics this book includes.

This book does not treat Agile as a religion that requires an elevated state of consciousness, but as a collection of specific management and technical practices whose effects and interactions can be understood in business and technical terms.

This book provides a roadmap to modern Agile practices that work—and a few cautions about Agile practices and ideas to avoid. This book is not an Agile tutorial but a guide to help software leaders separate the signal from the noise.

CHAPTER TWO

What's Really Different About Agile?

Most Agile books with a chapter title like "What's Really Different About Agile?" would immediately dive into historical descriptions of the 2001 Agile Manifesto and its related 20-year-old Agile Principles.

These documents served important and useful purposes 20 years ago, but Agile practices have continued to mature since then, and neither of these historic references accurately characterize the most valuable aspects of Agile today.

So, what is different about Agile today? The Agile movement historically contrasted itself with waterfall development. The claim was that waterfall development tried to do 100% of its planning up front, 100% of its requirements work up front, 100% of its design up front, and so on. This was an accurate characterization of literal "waterfall" development, but it described a mode of development that was never actually in widespread use. Various kinds of *phased development* were common, but true waterfall development existed mainly in early US Department of Defense projects, and that early crude implementation had already been superseded by more sophisticated software lifecycles by the time the Agile Manifesto was written.[2]

The most meaningful contrast with Agile development today is *Sequential development.* Mischaracterizations aside, the contrasts are as shown in Table 2-1.

Short release cycles vs. long release cycles

Agile development typically delivers working software in cycles measured in days or weeks. Sequential development cycles are typically measured in months or quarters.

End-to-end development of small batches vs. large batches

Agile development emphasizes complete development—including detailed requirements, design, coding, and testing—in small batches, meaning a small number of features or requirements at a time. Sequential development emphasizes moving an entire project's worth of requirements, design, coding, and testing through the development pipeline at the same time in large batches. Agile development is like a dashed line. Sequential development is like a series of parallel lines.

---

[2] MIL-STD-2167A was superseded by MIL-STD-498 at the end of 1994.

Table 2-1 Differences Between Agile Development and Sequential Development

Agile Development	Sequential Development
Short release cycles	Long release cycles
Most end-to-end development work performed in small batches within release cycles	Most end-to-end development work performed in large batches across entire release cycles
High-level up-front planning with just-in-time detailed planning	Detailed up-front planning
High-level up-front requirements with just-in-time detailed requirements	Detailed up-front requirements
Emergent design	Up-front design
Continuous testing, integrated into development	Test at the end, often as separate activity
Frequent structured collaboration	Infrequent structured collaboration
OODA as improvement model	PDCA as improvement model

Up-front planning vs. just-in-time planning

Agile development typically does only a little planning up front and leaves most of the detailed planning to be done just in time. Well-done Sequential development also does a lot of its planning just in time, but Sequential practices such as earned value put a stronger emphasis on planning in more detail up front.

Up-front requirements vs. just-in-time requirements

Agile development focuses on doing as little requirements work as possible up front (emphasizing breadth rather than depth); it delays the vast majority of detailed requirements work until it is needed after the project is underway. Sequential development focuses on getting as many requirements details as possible well-understood and well-defined up front.

This is an area in which there has been an evolution of Agile requirements practices, and modern Agile practices have moved beyond the ideas that were commonly associated with Agile 15 years ago.

Emergent design vs. up-front design

As with planning and requirements, Agile defers detailed elaboration of design work until it is needed, with minimal emphasis on up-front architecture. Sequential development emphasizes developing a greater level of detail up front.

The acknowledgment of value in *some* up-front design and architecture work is another area in which modern Agile has moved beyond the Agile philosophy of the early 2000s.

Continuous, integrated testing vs. separate test at the end

Agile development emphasizes testing as something that is done concurrently with coding, sometimes preceding coding. It is performed by integrated development teams that include both developers and test specialists. Sequential development treats testing as an activity that is done separately from development, and typically after development has occurred.

Frequent structured collaboration vs. infrequent unstructured collaboration

Agile development emphasizes frequent, structured collaboration. These collaborations are often short (15-minute daily standup meeting), but they are structured into the day-by-day, week-by-week rhythm of Agile work. Sequential development certainly does not prevent collaboration, but it doesn't particularly support it. When collaborations occur, they are either less frequent (formal design review meetings) or less structured (informal design discussions at a whiteboard).

OODA vs. PDCA as improvement model

Agile teams emphasize an empirical approach. They focus on learning from real-world experience. Sequential teams try to learn from experience too, but they place greater emphasis on defining a plan and imposing order on reality, rather than observing reality and constantly adapting to it. (I'll describe OODA and PDCA in Chapter 3.)

What Agile and Sequential Development Have in Common

Comparisons of Agile and Sequential tend to compare good Agile to bad Sequential, or vice versa. This is not fair or useful. On well-run projects, good management, a high level of customer collaboration, and high-quality requirements, design, coding and testing are common to both Agile and Sequential approaches.

Sequential development at its best can work well. However, if you study the differences described earlier in Table 2-1 and reflect on your own projects, you'll see some hints about why Agile has worked better than Sequential development in so many cases.

What Do You Mean by Agile?

As I mentioned earlier, the term "Agile" has become an all-inclusive umbrella term that encompasses better and worse practices, frameworks, principles, and values. One consequence of this loose terminology is that when someone refers to "going Agile," it's difficult for others to know what they mean. I've seen people have extended conversations about "Agile" without realizing that they're talking about completely non-overlapping concepts.

If an organization intends to go Agile, it should define what it means by "Agile." Does it mean:

- Release software into production many times an hour with no downtime?
- Accommodate occasional late changes in a regulated system without compromising quality and safety?
- Restore a service outage in an average of minutes?
- Respond successfully on the software side to late changes on the hardware side?
- Support a blue/green deployment environment?
- Succeed on large projects or with multi-site development?
- Support the business itself becoming more Agile?
- Improve quality, cycle time, throughput or productivity generally?

We have worked with companies that had each of these objectives—the practices that will work best for you will vary significantly depending on your specific goals.

What Is the Source of Agile's Benefits?

The benefits of Agile development do not arise from a mystical application of the term "Agile." They come from easily explainable benefits of the Agile emphases listed in Table 2-1.

Short release cycles allow for more timely and less expensive correction of defects, more rapid customer feedback, faster course corrections, and less time invested in dead ends.

End-to-end development work performed in small batches provides benefits for similar reasons—tighter feedback loops, allowing errors to be detected and corrected more quickly, at lower cost.

Just-in-time planning results in less time spent creating detailed plans that are later ignored or thrown away.

Just-in-time requirements results in less work invested in up-front requirements work that is eventually discarded when requirements change.

Emergent design results in less work invested in designing up-front solutions for requirements that later change. Up-front design can be powerful, but up-front design for speculative requirements is error-prone and wasteful.

Continuous testing is another way in which Agile practices tighten the feedback loop between the time a defect is inserted and the time it's detected, contributing to lower-cost defect corrections.

Frequent, structured collaboration reduces the communication mistakes that can contribute significantly to defects in requirements, design, and other activities.

OODA as an improvement model encourages the teams to learn from experience and improve over time.

These benefits are readily available to any organization that develops skill in using the practices that embody these emphases.

Different organizations will consider different factors as they decide which emphases to adopt. An organization that develops life-critical software will typically not adopt emergent design. Emergent design might save money, but safety considerations are more important.

Similarly, an organization that incurs a high cost each time it releases its software—perhaps because it's embedded in a difficult-to-access device or because of regulatory overhead—will not choose to release often. The feedback obtained by releasing often might save some organizations money, but it might cost other organizations more than it saves.

Once you move beyond the thinking that "Agile" is an irreducible concept that must be applied *all-or-nothing*, you become free to adopt the specific Agile practices that are best-suited to your organization. If your organization needs to support business agility, modern Agile software practices are a natural fit. If your organization needs to support quality, predictability, productivity, or some other not-obviously-Agile attribute, modern Agile software practices are also valuable.

The Agile Boundary

Most organizations cannot achieve end-to-end agility. Your organization might not see any benefit from Agile HR or Agile procurement. Even if you commit to agility organization-wide, you might find that your customers are less Agile or your suppliers are.

It is useful to understand where the boundary is between Agile and non-Agile parts of your organization—both the current boundary and the desired boundary.

If you're a C-level executive, the area inside the Agile boundary could include your entire organization. If you're the top technical leader in your organization, it could include your entire organization. If you're a lower-level leader in your organization, the area inside the Agile boundary might include only your teams.

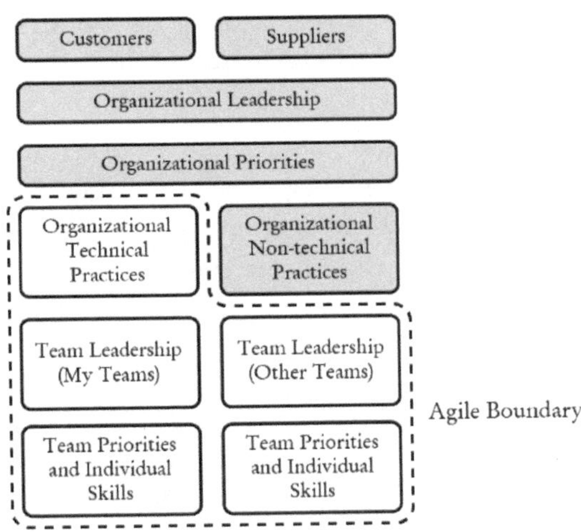

Figure 2-5
Example of an Agile boundary. In this example, Agile practices are limited to the technical organization.

Every organization has a boundary, even if it's with a non-Agile customer. How thoroughly do you want to implement Agile in your organization? What will best serve your business?

Suggested Leadership Actions

Inspect

- Review your project portfolio in terms of the factors described in Table 2-1. Investigate your average release cycle length, your focus on completing features in small batches vs. all at the same time, the ratio of up-front planning to just-in-time planning, the ratio of up-front requirements work to just-in-time work, your use of emergent design vs. up-front design, support for collaboration, and the approach to quality assurance (QA) and testing.
- Talk to at least three technical leaders in your organization. Ask them what they mean by "Agile." Ask them what specific practices they are referring to. To what degree do your technical leaders agree on what Agile means?

Adapt

- Based on the information gathering suggested above and using the criteria in Table 2-1, score the Agility of each of your projects on a scale of 1–5 (from least Agile to most Agile).
- Write down a preliminary approach to drawing the "Agile boundary" in your organization.
- Write a list of questions to answer as you read the rest of this book.

Additional Resources

Stellman, Andrew and Jennifer Green. 2013. *Learning Agile: Understanding Scrum, XP, Lean, and Kanban.* s.l. : O'Reilly Media, 2013.

CHAPTER THREE

From PDCA to OODA

In some key respects the difference between Sequential and Agile development can be summed up as a difference in focus between PDCA and OODA.

"PDCA" is an acronym that stands for Plan Do Check Act and is normally described as the "PDCA cycle." This approach is associated with W. Edwards Deming, and it essentially means what it sounds like it means. It's a methodical approach to planning, performing work, observing results, analyzing the effectiveness of changes, and then incorporating learnings into the next cycle.

"OODA" stands for Observe, Orient, Decide, Act and is normally described as the "OODA loop." The OODA loop was invented by US Air Force Colonel John Boyd to improve the success rate of United States Air Force pilots in dog fights. OODA is a methodical approach to establishing context, formulating a plan, performing work, observing results, and incorporating learnings into the next cycle.

PDCA and OODA are similar, but they differ in a few key respects.

PDCA

In PDCA, improvement begins with "Plan." This is an analytical activity in which you map out what you're going to do, potentially in significant detail. In Sequential development, the Planning includes project planning, product planning, and process planning. Requirements, architecture, and design are all performed to a significant degree before the "Do" activity of software construction begins.

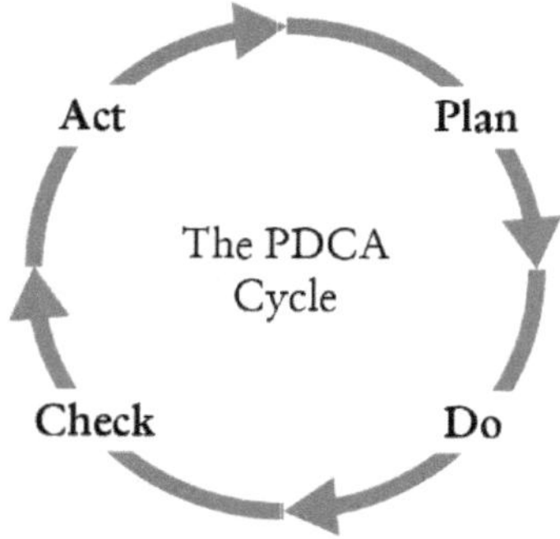

Figure 3-1

The PDCA cycle is a four-step management method that begins with planning.

The next step is "Do," meaning carry out the plan. In Sequential development this consists of construction and testing, which follows through on the project management and technical plans made previously and which follows the process defined previously.

You then "Check"—you compare the actual output to the expected output and look for similarities and differences. You also look for how well your plan worked compared to previous plans.

In the "Act" phase, you revise your approach depending on whether your plan worked better or worse than previous approaches. If it worked better, you make that plan the new baseline. If it worked worse, you revert to an earlier plan as the baseline.

There are numerous ways to apply PDCA variations to software projects. You can apply PDCA at the whole project level, within individual activities (such as requirements work), or within vertical slices of work (an individual feature completion effort). PDCA is intended to be iterative, which is why it's called the PDCA *cycle*. But the basic characterization remains—the cycle begins with planning.

OODA

OODA originated out of Colonel John Boyd's frustration with US Air Force dog fighting results. He invented the OODA loop as a way to accelerate decision making, make decisions faster than the enemy, and invalidate the enemy's decision making.

In the OODA loop approach, the loop begins with "Observe." Observe the current situation, observe outside information that's relevant, observe any aspects of the situation that are "unfolding" (emergent), and observe how the unfolding aspects of the situation are interacting with the environment. Because OODA places so much emphasis on observation, you can think of OODA as an empirical approach—an approach that focuses on observation and experience.

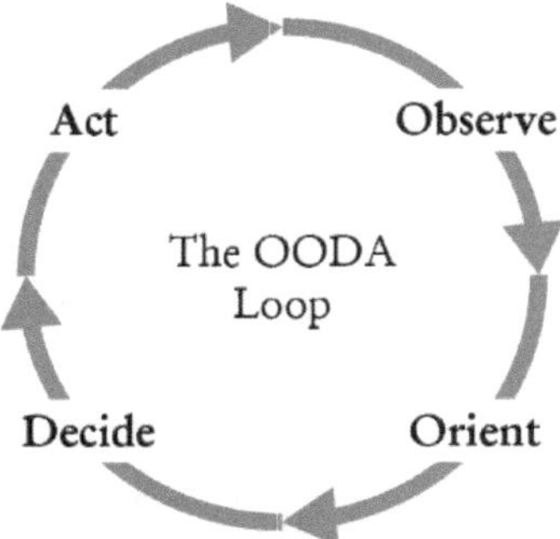

Figure 3-2
The OODA loop also contains four steps, but it begins with observation rather than planning.

In the "Orient" step, you relate the observations to your situation. Boyd stated that we relate them to our "genetic heritage, cultural tradition, and previous experiences" (Wikipedia, 2018). Put less ethereally, you decide what the information means to you and you identify the options that are available to you in response. The "Orient" step is often the make-or-break step in the OODA loop. This is where you overlook details that turn out to be important or you misinterpret them. Or you realize the significance of details that others have overlooked. Apple's iPhone is a classic example. The rest of the wireless handset industry was focused on megapixels in the camera, RF signal quality, and battery life. Apple oriented in a completely different way, focusing on creating a mobile information appliance with a groundbreaking UX. The iPhone was inferior in almost every respect *as a traditional mobile phone*, but that didn't matter because Apple had oriented toward solving a different problem that was ultimately more important.

In the "Decide" step, you make a decision based on the options you identified during the "Orient" step. In a military context, you often decide to do something that disrupts your adversary's plans or approach. This is called "getting inside the opponent's OODA loop." Although this is sometimes interpreted as operating faster than your adversary, it's really just operating at a different tempo than your adversary. For example, a baseball pitcher who throws a change-up when the batter is expecting a fast ball is effectively getting inside his adversary's OODA loop by operating more slowly.

Finally, you "Act" by implementing the decision. And then you immediately jump back to "Observe" so that you can see the impact of your action and begin the OODA loop again.

It's been observed that PDCA and OODA are essentially the same idea, with one of the cycles rotated one-quarter turn from the other. In practice, the key difference between OODA and PDCA is that OODA begins with observation rather than planning, which fundamentally changes the approach from one of imposing order on the environment to one of assessing what kind of action will be effective in the environment.

What this means in Sequential vs. Agile development is that in Sequential (PDCA) you have big planning up front, big design up front, and so on. In Agile (OODA) you have just-in-time planning, requirements, design, and implementation within iterative release cycles. PDCA can be seen as more predictive, OODA as more reactive. Agile development does not try to anticipate as much as Sequential does.

Another difference is what happens when you begin your second pass through the PDCA cycle or OODA loop. When you begin the OODA loop for the second time, you begin, again, by observing. This allows you to assess whether the circumstances have changed since the last time you observed. When you plan at the beginning of a second PDCA cycle, you implicitly assume that nothing has changed except what you have intended to change. Because OODA makes no assumptions about what might or might not have changed, it has been found to be a more responsive model for use in an ever-changing world.

A final difference is the attitude toward uncertainty. PDCA views uncertainty as risk—as something you need to reduce or eliminate. OODA views uncertainty as opportunity—as something you can exploit to gain an advantage over your adversary.

Key Principle: Inspect and Adapt

I find the phrase "Inspect and Adapt" a useful shorthand for OODA and also a useful shorthand for appropriate, effective focus in Agile development. Agile teams should avoid being idealistic about their practices and instead adjust their practices based on empirical observations about what actually works. Agile teams should be regularly Inspecting and Adapting *everything*—plans, designs, processes, team interactions, organizational interactions—every factor that can make a difference in a team's effectiveness.

The "Suggested Leadership Actions" at the end of each chapter in this book emphasize the value of this principle.

Suggested Leadership Actions

Inspect

- Reflect on the PDCA cycle and OODA loop concepts. Do your projects and releases seem like they are amenable to a linear up-front planning and execution approach, or would they benefit from a more exploratory approach? Are they a mix, or are they all pretty similar?
- Review your organization's approach to improvement. Is it based more on PDCA or more on OODA? How well does the approach match your project types?
- To what degree are your projects using Inspect and Adapt? When and where else could you use Inspect and Adapt?
- In OODA terms, *Observe* who your "adversary" is (specific competitor, market share, profit goal, etc.).
- *Observe* 3–5 areas of uncertainty that you could potentially exploit to gain advantage over your adversary.

Adapt

- *Orient* using the areas of uncertainty in ways that will provide advantages over your adversary.
- *Decide* how to take advantage of your insights into uncertainty and then *Act*.

Additional Resources

The OODA loop concept goes far beyond the sketch I've provided in this chapter. Here are some sources that offer much more detail.

Boyd, John R. 2007. *Patterns of Conflict.* January 2007. This is a re-creation of a briefing presented by Col. John Boyd, as created by him around December 1986 and updated to account for changes he made by hand after that.

Coram, Robert. 2002. *Boyd: The Fighter Pilot Who Changed the Art of War*. New York : Back Bay Books, 2002. This is an in-depth biography of Col. John Boyd.

Richards, Chet. 2004. *Certain to Win: The Strategy of John Boyd, Applied to Business.* s.l. : Xlibris Corporation, 2004. This book is a readable description of the origin of the OODA loop and applications to business decision making.

Wikipedia. 2018. OODA Loop. Wikipedia. [Online] November 28, 2018. [Cited: November 28, 2018.] https://en.wikipedia.org/wiki/OODA_loop. The Wikipedia article on OODA provides a good basic explanation but does not describe Col. Boyd's original motivation for creating OODA.

CHAPTER FOUR

Cynefin, PDCA, and OODA

Another useful framework for dealing with uncertain circumstances is the Cynefin framework (pronounced kuh-NEV-in), created by David Snowden (Snowden, 2007). Cynefin is a way to make sense of complexity and uncertainty, and as such it's useful for making sense of software projects.

The Cynefin framework consists of five domains, illustrated in Figure 4-1 and described in the following sections.

Obvious Domain

In the Obvious domain (sometimes also called the Simple domain), problems are well understood and solutions are self-evident. Literally everyone agrees on the one correct answer.

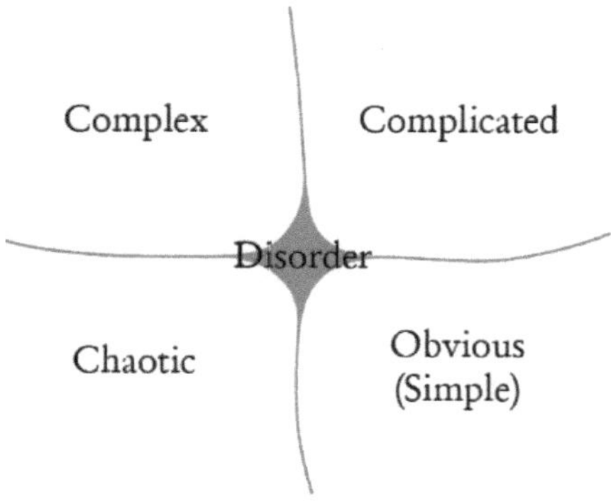

Figure 4-1
The Cynefin framework is a useful sense-making framework that can be applied to software development.

In the Obvious domain, the relationship between cause and effect is simple, direct, and completely understood. This is the realm of pattern application: programmed, proceduralized, rote behavior.

The approach to Obvious problems is described in the framework as

sense ● *categorize* ● *respond*

Examples of actions in the Obvious domain include:

- Taking an order at a restaurant
- Processing a loan payment
- Installing a software upgrade (sometimes)

In software, at the detailed level there are numerous Obvious problems, such as, "This story is too big and needs to be split into multiple stories." At the project level it's difficult to find examples of Obvious problems, as defined in Cynefin. When's the last time you saw a problem of any size in software that had only one correct answer and for which everyone agreed on the solution? There's good research in software that says when different designers are presented with the same design problem, they will create solutions that vary by a factor of 10 in code volume needed to implement their designs (McConnell, 2004). This is about as far from one correct solution as you can get. So, beyond a "hello world" program, I don't believe that Obvious problems exist in software development. As far as software is concerned I believe you can safely ignore the Obvious domain.

Complicated Domain

In the Complicated domain, you know the general shape of the problem, what questions to ask, and how to obtain answers. Also, multiple correct answers exist. The relationship between cause and effect is complicated—you have to analyze, investigate, and apply expert knowledge to understand the relationship between cause and effect. Not everyone can see or understand the cause/effect relationships, which makes Complicated the domain of experts.

The approach to Complicated problems is described in Cynefin as

sense • analyze • respond

This approach is a contrast to the approach in the Obvious domain, in that the middle step requires *analysis* rather than simply *classifying* the problem and choosing the one correct response.

Examples of actions in the Complicated domain include:

- Diagnose an engine knock sound
- Prepare a gourmet meal

- Write a database query to obtain a certain result
- Fix a bug in a production system that resulted from an incomplete update
- Prioritize user requirements for version 4.1 of a mature system

What these examples have in common is that first you formulate an understanding of the problem and a plan to attack the problem, and then you move in a linear way toward solving the problem.

Numerous software development activities and software projects fall into the Complicated domain. Historically, this is the realm of Sequential development.

Complex Domain

The defining characteristic of the Complex domain is that the relationship between cause and effect is not immediately apparent, even to experts. In contrast to the Complicated domain, you don't know all the questions to ask. Part of the challenge is discovering the questions. No amount of advance analysis will solve the problem, and experimentation is required to progress toward a solution. In fact, some amount of failure is part of the process, and decisions will often need to be made on the basis of incomplete data.

For Complex problems, the relationship between cause and effect is knowable only in hindsight—certain elements of the problem are emergent. However, with enough experimentation, the relationship between cause and effect can become known well enough to support practical decision making. Snowden says that Complex problems are the realm of collaboration, patience, and allowing solutions to emerge.

The recommended approach to Complex problems is described in Cynefin as

probe • sense • respond

This is a contrast to Complicated problems in that, for Complex problems, you can't analyze your way out of the problem. You have to probe first. Eventually, analysis will become relevant, but not immediately.

Examples of problems in the Complex domain include:

- Buying a gift for someone who is difficult to shop for (you give the gift knowing that you will need to exchange it!)
- Fixing a bug in a production system in which diagnostic tools make the bug disappear
- Eliciting user requirements for a brand new system
- Creating software that runs on underlying hardware that's still evolving
- Updating your software while competitors are updating their software

Many software development activities and projects fall into the Complex domain, and this is the realm of Agile and iterative development. Sequential development's failure to do well on Complex projects is, in my view, a substantial part of what gave rise to Agile development.

In some cases, you can probe a predominately Complex project in enough detail up front to turn it into a Complicated project—the remainder of the project can then be conducted using approaches that are appropriate for Complicated projects. In other cases, a Complex project retains significant Complex elements throughout its project lifecycle. An attempt to convert the project to Complicated wastes time that would be better spent completing the project using approaches appropriate for Complex projects.

Chaotic Domain

The Chaotic domain departs a bit from the pattern you might expect based on the first three domains. In the Chaotic domain, the relationship between cause and effect is turbulent and in flux. There's no discoverable relationship between cause and effect even with repeated experimentation, even in hindsight. You don't know the questions to ask, and probes and experiments do not produce consistent responses.

The domain also includes a time-pressure element not present in the other domains.

Cynefin defines the Chaotic domain as the domain of decisive, action-oriented leadership. The recommended approach is to impose order on chaos and to do it quickly:

act • sense • respond

Examples of Chaotic problems include:

- Providing hurricane relief while the hurricane is still happening
- Stopping a food fight in a high school cafeteria
- Fixing a bug in a production system by rolling back to a previous version because no amount of analysis or probing has found the cause of the bug
- Defining a feature set when customer feedback suggests significant changes to the overall direction every time you show the working software

Finding project-size examples of Chaotic problems in software is difficult or impossible. The bug fix example has the "no time to think, just act" element, but it isn't a project-size example. The feature set example doesn't have the extreme time-pressure element, which means that it isn't a completely representative example of a Chaotic problem in Cynefin terms.

Disorder Domain

The middle of the Cynefin diagram is described as Disorder, which Cynefin defines as what happens when you lack clarity about which domain applies to your problem.

In Cynefin, different elements of a problem or system can exhibit different attributes—some parts might be Complicated while others are Complex. Cynefin's recommended approach to Disorder is to decompose the problem into its elements and then assess which domain each element is in.

Most software project-size problems are not tidily divided into one domain, so keep in mind that Cynefin is a Welsh word that means "habitat" or "neighborhood" rather than "strict categorization." Cynefin's domains are collections of meanings that cluster together. Any given problem might not be cleanly all Complicated or all Complex, but it might reside more in the "neighborhood" of Complex than Complicated.

In software-intensive systems today, it's all but certain that the problems we are trying to solve will have some elements that are Complicated and others that are Complex. One value of Cynefin is providing a way to identify these different elements and treat each appropriately. You approach requirements, design, and planning work one way in the

Complex domain and a different way in the Complicated domain. A single approach does not work everywhere.

Complicated and Complex Domains, PDCA, and OODA

Cynefin is an interesting and useful sense-making framework, and all five domains apply to problems outside of software. For software projects, however, the Chaotic and Obvious domains don't apply at the whole-project level for the reasons described above. That means, for practical purposes, software projects should orient themselves as being mostly in the Complicated, Complex, or Disorder domains.

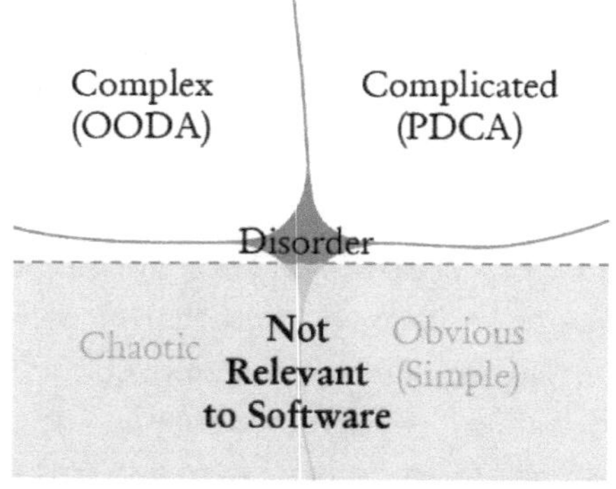

Figure 4-2

The relationship between Cynefin's domains, PDCA, and OODA.

Combining ideas from Cynefin, PDCA, and OODA provides useful insight into how to approach a software project. If the project is mostly in the Complicated realm, an approach that relies more heavily on up-front planning and analysis can work—because the problem is well-defined. This is the domain of PDCA.

If the project is mostly in the Complex realm, a workable approach will need to build in experimentation and probing before the problem can even be fully defined. This is the domain of OODA.

Considering that you have only two choices of domains in Cynefin, it's useful to ask the question, "What if I guess wrong about my project's domain?"

If you believe your project is mostly Complex and it turns out to be only Complicated, you will have spent time on probing and experimentation that you didn't need to. The penalty for guessing wrong in this case is a less efficient project—although that's arguable because the experiments you performed probably increased your understanding of your project and improved how you approached it.

If you believe your project is mostly Complicated and it turns out to be mostly Complex, you will have spent time analyzing, planning, and probably at least partially executing a project that you didn't understand as well as you thought you did. If you're one month into a six-month project when you discover your mission was actually something different, a complete restart of the project might be necessary. If you're five months into a six-month project, the project could be cancelled outright. Your business might not be able to justify repeating its investment in that area, or you might have lost the business opportunity because of the five-month delay.

The consequence of guessing wrong is lower for guessing a project is Complex than for guessing it's Complicated. The safe money, therefore, goes into treating a project as Complex (and therefore calling for an OODA approach) unless you can be absolutely sure that it's Complicated. And there aren't all that many cases in software development where we can have that degree of clarity.

The software problems that companies are addressing today have many cross-cutting, emergent characteristics that are not naturally addressed by Sequential approaches. Agile practices provide a better fit for these problems, with better risk management and softer failure modes.

Suggested Leadership Actions

Inspect

- Review your current projects. Which elements of your projects would you describe as Complex, and which would you describe as Complicated?
- Review a recent challenged project in your organization. Did your teams treat important aspects of the project as though they were Complicated or Complex? Does it appear that any of those projects' challenges might have arisen from a Complex project being misclassified as Complicated (or possibly vice versa)?
- Review a project that has been cancelled or that went through a major replanning. How many months into the project were problems discovered? Would treating any aspects of that project as Complex—probing more at the beginning and applying the OODA loop way of thinking—have made a difference in its outcome? Would it have resulted in discovering problems earlier (saving time and effort)?

Adapt

- Create a list of projects that your organization should be treating as Complex rather than Complicated. Work with your project teams to begin treating them that way.

Additional Resources

Snowden, David J. and Mary E. Boone. 2007. A Leader's Framework for Decision Making. *Harvard Business Review.* November 2007.

A Spiral Model of Software Development and Enhancement. Boehm, Barry W. 1988. s.l. : Computer, May 1988. In Cynefin terms, this paper proposes an approach to projects in which each project is initially treated as Complex. Issues are probed until the project's complete set of challenges is understood well enough to treat the project as Complicated. At that point, the project is completed as a Sequential project.

More Effective Agile Projects

CHAPTER FIVE

More Effective Agile Beginnings: Scrum

It's human nature to want to begin with the most effective practices available. But beginners do not have the same skill sets as advanced practitioners, and that limits which practices will be most effective for beginners.

Key Principle: Start with Scrum

If you do not already have an Agile implementation—or if you have an Agile implementation that's less effective than you want it to be—I recommend that you begin at the beginning. In Agile, that means beginning with Scrum. And that is an exceedingly common approach—the *State of Scrum 2017–2018* report found that 84% of Agile adoptions included Scrum (Scrum Alliance, 2017).

What Is Scrum?

Scrum is a lightweight but structured workflow management approach for teams. Scrum doesn't dictate specific technical practices. It defines how the work will flow through a team, and it dictates some specific roles and work-coordination practices that the team will use.

Scrum Basics

If you're familiar with Scrum basics, feel free to skip this section and move on to this chapter's "Common Failure Modes in Scrum" section or, if those are also familiar, to "Success Factors in Scrum." The most canonical description of Scrum is normally considered to be *The Scrum Guide* (Schwaber, 2017). My company's experience with Scrum mostly matches what's described in *The Scrum Guide*, so the following description mostly follows the November 2017 version of the *Guide* (but not completely).

Scrum is often summarized as having events (also known as meetings or ceremonies), roles, and artifacts that are bound together with a set of rules.

Scrum begins, conceptually, with a "product backlog," which is created by the Product Owner. (I'll describe the Scrum roles in more detail below.) The product backlog is a set of stories, requirements, features, functions, enhancements, and fixes that the Scrum team might possibly deliver. ("Stories" are the most common kind of requirement in Agile development.) Rather than providing a complete list of every possible requirement, the product backlog focuses on those requirements that are most important, that are most urgent, and that offer the highest ROI (return on investment).

The Scrum team performs its work in "sprints" or iterations, which are 1-to-4-week time-boxed blocks of work. Sprints of 1–2 weeks usually work best. We have found that risks increase with longer sprints and improvement opportunities are more limited. Two-week sprints are by far the most common.

Each sprint begins with a "sprint planning meeting," during which the team reviews the product backlog, selects a subset of the work to put into a sprint backlog, commits to deliver the items in the sprint backlog by the end of the sprint, and makes other plans needed to conduct the sprint. The team also defines a "sprint goal" that concisely captures the focus of the sprint. If work during a sprint unfolds in a way that surprises the team, the sprint goal provides a principled basis for renegotiating details of the sprint after work is underway.

The whole team works on design during sprint planning, which is effective because the team is cross-functional and has every discipline needed to make good decisions about design.

The team does not enter the sprint planning meeting "cold." The team performs work prior to the sprint planning meeting to refine requirements and design in enough detail to support the sprint planning meeting.

The functionality that the team delivers at the end of each sprint is called an "increment." In normal conversation, an "increment" would refer to only the additional functionality delivered in each sprint. In Scrum, however, "increment" refers to the aggregate of functionality developed to date.

During the sprint itself, the sprint backlog is considered to be a closed box. Requirements clarifications occur throughout the sprint, but no one can add, remove, or modify requirements that would imperil the sprint goal unless the Product Owner agrees to cancel the sprint and start the cycle over.

During the sprint, the team meets for a "daily scrum" (also known as a "daily standup"), which is held each day except the first and last day of the sprint. The daily scrum is timeboxed to 15 minutes. The focus is on inspecting progress toward the sprint goal. The content of the meeting is usually limited to answering "the three questions":

- What did you do yesterday?
- What will you do today?
- What is blocking progress?

Any discussion other than these three questions is normally deferred until after the standup, although some teams use a more discussion-oriented approach.

The Scrum team follows the basic rhythm of daily scrum, daily work, daily scrum, daily work, rinse and repeat for the entire sprint. The team will often use a "sprint burndown chart" to track its progress during each sprint.

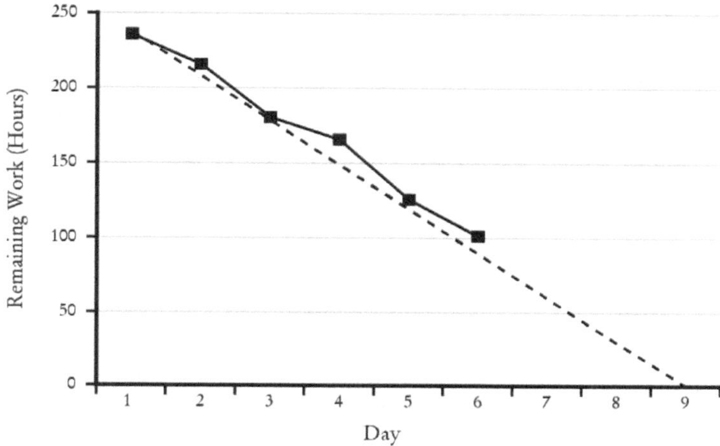

Figure 5-1
An example of a sprint burndown chart showing planned vs. actual hours remaining.

The focus of the sprint burndown chart is on hours remaining rather than hours consumed. If a task was planned to consume 8 hours and actually took 16 hours, the graph shows remaining work being reduced by only 8 hours. (This is essentially the same as Earned Value.) If the team's plans for the sprint are optimistic, the sprint burndown will show the remaining hours are not burning down as quickly as they should be.

When the organization values longer-term predictability, we also recommend that teams use a "release burndown chart" to track overall progress toward the current release. The release burndown nominally shows the total number of story points planned for the release, rate of progress to date, and a projection of when the release will be completed.

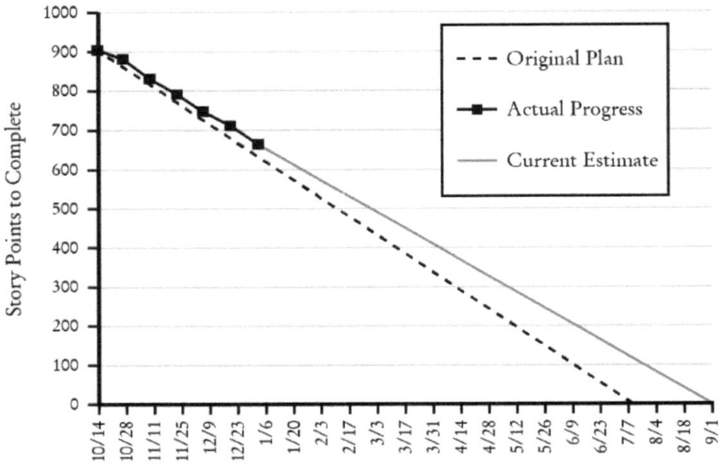

Figure 5-2

An example of a nominal release burndown chart.

More informative and elaborate burndowns are possible. They can be presented as burndowns or as burnups. They can show the history of the release's build-up of functionality, reductions in functionality, ranges of projected completion dates, and so on.

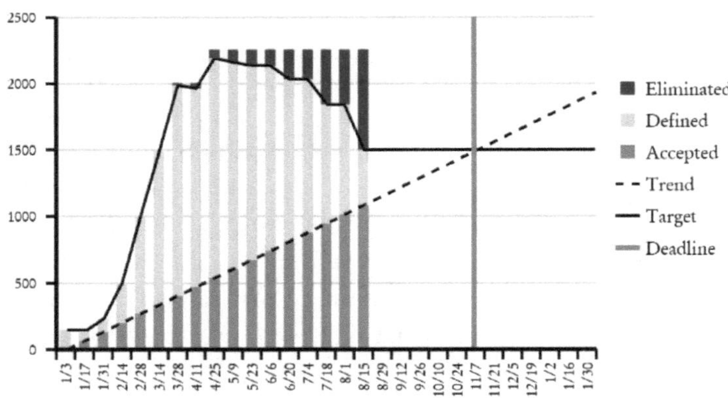

Figure 5-3

An example of a more elaborate release burndown chart.

Throughout the sprint, the team maintains high quality in its work. By the end of the sprint, the work must be at a "potentially releasable" level of quality that meets the team's "Definition of Done" (discussed later). The team does not need to actually release the software at the end of each sprint, but the quality must be good enough to support releasing what's been implemented each sprint, eventually, without further changes.

At the end of the sprint, the Scrum team invites project stakeholders to share perspectives and provide feedback. The Product Owner accepts or rejects items based upon the agreed-upon acceptance criteria as well as stakeholder feedback. The Scrum Master can reject items that fail to meet the Definition of Done. The team uses feedback obtained during the Sprint Review to improve the product as well as its processes and practices.

The final event of each sprint is a "sprint retrospective," at which the team reviews successes and failures of the sprint. This is the team's opportunity to use Inspect and Adapt to improve the process they're using to develop software. The team reviews any previous changes made and decides whether to continue with each change or reverse it. The team also agrees on new process changes to implement during the next sprint.

Figure 5-4 summarizes the flow of work on a Scrum project.

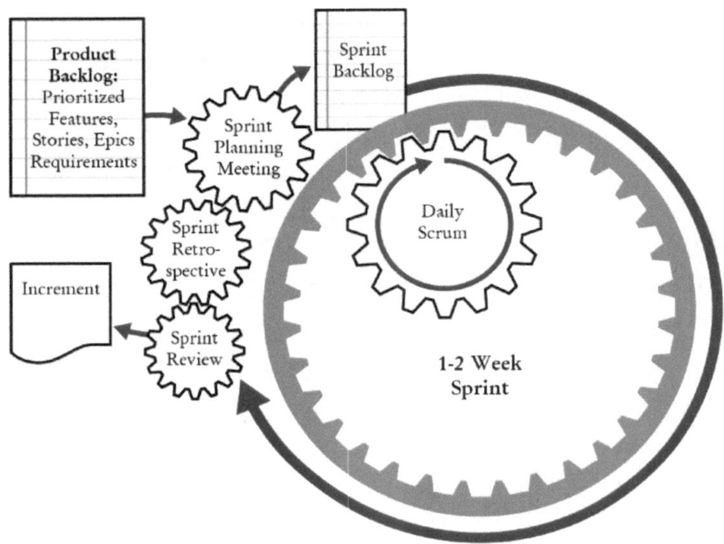

Figure 5-4
The flow of work through Scrum at a glance.

Scrum Roles

In support of the workflow on a Scrum project, three roles are defined.

The "Product Owner" is the interface between the Scrum team on the one hand and the business management, customers, and other stakeholders on the other. The Product Owner (or PO) has primary responsibility for defining the product backlog and prioritizing items in the product backlog, with the overarching responsibility of defining the product in a way that maximizes the value delivered by the Scrum team. The Product Owner regularly refines the product backlog so that it always contains about two sprints' worth of refined (fully defined) backlog items beyond the current sprint's backlog.

The "Scrum Master" is responsible for the Scrum implementation. The Scrum Master helps the team and larger organization understand Scrum theory, practice, and general approach. The Scrum Master manages the process, enforces the process if necessary, removes impediments, and coaches and supports the rest of the Scrum team.

The "Development Team" consists of the cross-functional individual contributors who directly do the work to implement the backlog items.

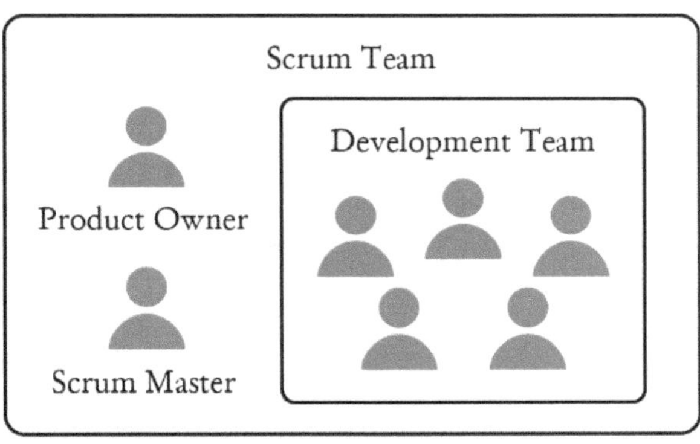

Figure 5-5
The organization of a Scrum team.

The overall Scrum team usually consists of 3–9 individuals on the Development Team plus the Scrum Master and Product Owner.

Common Failure Modes in Scrum

Scrum is a minimal process for managing workflow. Because it is already minimal, there really isn't any part of Scrum that you can remove and still achieve the benefits of Scrum.

> *"Perfection is achieved, not when there is nothing more to add, but when there is nothing left to take away."*
> —Antoine de Saint-Exupery

My company has seen many more ineffective Scrum implementations than effective ones. Most ineffective implementations are "Scrum But," meaning, "We're doing Scrum, *but* we aren't doing daily standups." Or "We're doing Scrum, *but* we aren't holding retrospectives." Or "We're doing Scrum, *but* we haven't been able to fill the Product Owner role." Ineffective Scrum implementations have usually removed at least one essential attribute of Scrum. My favorite example was a company that said, "We looked at Scrum but found that most of the practices wouldn't work in our organization. We're doing Scrum, but the main practice we use is daily standups, and we do those on Fridays."

If your organization has adopted Scrum and you aren't realizing significant benefits, the first question to ask is, Have you really adopted Scrum, or have you adopted only parts of Scrum? An advanced Scrum implementation might eventually remove specific parts of Scrum by applying Inspect and Adapt to their Scrum process with rigor. But that is an advanced activity, not a beginner activity. Beginners will do better if they adopt Scrum *by the book*.

The following sections describe the most common challenges we see with Scrum implementations.

Ineffective Product Owner

For decades before Agile development existed, the most commonly reported source of project challenges and failures was poor requirements. It should not be a surprise that post-Agile the most problematic role on Scrum projects is the one that's responsible for requirements.

Problems with Product Owners take several forms:

- No Product Owner—the role is expected to be filled by individuals on the Scrum team.
- The PO is spread too thin—this starves the Scrum team for requirements.
- The PO doesn't adequately understand the business—this results in low-quality requirements being fed to the Scrum team or requirements that are prioritized poorly.
- The PO does not understand how to specify software requirements—this is another way that low quality requirements are fed to the Scrum team.
- The PO is not co-located with the rest of the Scrum team—the rest of the team cannot get timely answers to requirements questions.
- The PO has an agenda that differs from the business's—the team is sent in directions the business ultimately rejects.
- The PO refuses to abide by Scrum rules—this forces changes in requirements mid-sprint or otherwise disrupts the Scrum project.

Many of the problems with the Product Owner arise from businesses not taking the PO role as seriously as they take the Development Team and Scrum Master roles. Businesses should treat the PO as the highest-leverage role on a Scrum team and prioritize filling the role accordingly. With appropriate training, former business analysts, customer support staff, and testers can all make excellent POs.

Insufficient Product Backlog Refinement

The product backlog is used to feed work to the Development Team in Scrum. The Product Owner is responsible for the product backlog, and backlog refinement needs to be an ongoing activity so that the team is never starved for work.

Backlog refinement (also sometimes known as "backlog grooming") includes fleshing out stories in sufficient detail to support implementation of the stories, splitting stories that are too large to fit into one sprint into smaller stories, adding new stories, updating the relative priorities of different backlog items, estimating or re-estimating stories, and so on. In general, refining the backlog consists of filling in all the details the Scrum team will need to begin implementing a sprint's worth of backlog items at the next sprint.

Insufficient backlog refinement can cause a number of problems for the Scrum team. A well-refined product backlog is such a make-or-break issue for Agile projects that it is discussed at much greater length in Chapter 10, "More Effective Agile Requirements Creation," and Chapter 11, "More Effective Agile Requirements Prioritization."

Backlog refinement is nominally a whole-team activity. But because the Product Owner is responsible for the product backlog, if a project falls prey to the preceding pitfall of inadequately staffing the Product Owner role, it will typically fall prey to poor backlog refinement too.

Not Driving to a Potentially Releasable Level of Quality Each Sprint

One of the consequences of excessive schedule pressure is that teams and individuals will place the appearance of progress above actual progress. Because quality is less visible than basic functionality, teams under pressure sometimes emphasize quantity of work over quality. They might implement the functionality contained in their sprint backlog but not perform the testing, create automated tests, or otherwise assure that the software has been developed to a potentially releasable level of quality.

This leads to them declaring work to be "done" while some tasks are still incomplete.

The discipline of frequently driving software to a potentially releasable level of quality supports two important goals.

The first goal is to assure a high level of quality. The more often the software is driven to a high level of quality, the easier it is to maintain it at that level.

The second goal is to support project planning and tracking. If software is driven to a potentially releasable level of quality by the end of each sprint, that implies that there is no more work to do on that functionality later. If software is not driven to a potentially releasable level of quality, that means an undetermined amount of additional quality work must be done later. Quality work accumulates across sprints, which undermines the ability to determine the true status of the project. This important dynamic is discussed in more detail in Chapter 9, "More Effective Agile Quality."

For both these reasons, it is important for teams to drive their work to a potentially releasable level of quality at the end of each and every sprint.

Unclear Definition of Done

One important support for maintaining high quality is to have a rigorous "Definition of Done" (DoD). This helps to ensure that when an individual or team declares an item to be "done," the team and organization can be truly sure that no more work remains for that item. DoD is effectively an exit criteria that defines the standard that work must meet to be released into production or into the next downstream integration or testing phase. This is discussed in more detail in Chapter 9, "More Effective Agile Quality."

Emphasis on Horizontal Slices Rather than Vertical Slices

The term "vertical slice" refers to end-to-end functionality across the full technology stack. The term "horizontal slice" refers to an enabling capability that doesn't directly produce demonstrable business-level functionality.

Vertical slices are typically easier for nontechnical stakeholders to understand, observe, and assess for business value. They create options for the team to release sooner and realize actual business value and real user feedback.

Teams that focus on horizontal slices can go off into the weeds for several sprints at a time, working on stories that are in some sense "productive" but that don't produce observable business value.

Another effect of horizontal slices is that they can cause each team member to work independently, depriving the team of Scrum's group dynamic benefits.

We have found that the more successful Agile projects tend to drive each user story to production quality before moving on to the next user story, and less successful projects don't.

Horizontal vs. vertical slicing is an important topic that is discussed in more detail in Chapter 7, "More Effective Agile Projects."

Stories Too Large

In support of driving work to a releasable state by the end of each sprint, most stories should be completeable within a single sprint. There aren't any hard-and-fast rules in this area, but here are two useful guidelines:

- The team should decompose its stories so that no single story consumes more than half the team for half the sprint; most stories should be smaller.
- The team should aim to complete 6–12 stories each sprint.

The overall goal is to have the team completing stories throughout the sprint—not just on the last couple of days, but all along the way.

Overly Long Sprints

The current best practice is 1-to-2-week sprints, with most teams gravitating toward 2 weeks. When sprints are done less often than biweekly, too much space opens up for planning mistakes, overly optimistic sprint commitments, and so on.

Daily Scrums Not Held Daily

Daily scrums can become repetitive, and so some teams evolve toward holding them three times a week—sometimes even just one time per week. However, it is important to hold the daily scrums *daily* to give team members the opportunity to coordinate work, ask for help, and hold each other accountable.

The most common reason we hear for holding daily scrums less than daily is, "The meetings take too long." This is a clear identification of a problem! The meetings are supposed to be time-boxed to 15 minutes, and if the meetings stay focused on the three questions, they can be completed in that amount of time. The solution to overly long daily scrums is not to reduce the number of meetings; it's to keep the meetings time-boxed and focused on the three questions. (The current *Scrum Guide* has deprecated the role of the three questions, but I think they provide important structure and help to avoid poorly run meetings.)

Separate Development and Test Teams

A common holdover from Sequential development is to have separate development and test teams. This structure deprives the Scrum team of cross-functional expertise that it needs to operate effectively.

Retrospectives Not Held

When teams feel overwhelmed by the amount of work they're responsible for, they often skip retrospectives. This is a huge mistake! You won't escape the vicious cycle of over-commitment and burnout unless you give yourself an opportunity to learn from the planning and commitment mistakes that led to that cycle in the first place.

Agile development depends on application of the Inspect and Adapt cycle, and Scrum gives your teams regular opportunities to do that.

Lessons from Retrospectives Not Implemented in the Next Sprint

The final failure mode we see most commonly is holding the sprint retrospective but not actually implementing lessons learned in the next sprint. Lessons accumulate to be implemented "later," or retrospectives become a gripe session rather than one that's truly focused on taking corrective action.

Don't live with your problems—do something about them. Most of the problems we have seen affecting teams' ability to deliver has been addressable by the teams. Support your teams in taking corrective actions through retrospectives, and you'll be amazed at how quickly they improve.

What the Scrum Failure Modes Have in Common

The failure modes I've just described are all variations on the theme of Scrum But. The first order of business for a team or organization that is adopting Agile development is to ensure that it is making high-fidelity use of Scrum.

Most of these failure modes have another attribute in common, which is the failure to consistently use high-discipline practices. A "high-discipline" practice is a practice that people tend to drift away from unless there's social or structural support in place to make sure the practice occurs.

The Scrum Master is responsible for ensuring the high-discipline practices in Scrum (as well as the other practices). The meetings in Scrum—sprint planning, daily scrum, sprint review, and sprint retrospective—provide both social and structural support for the high-discipline practices.

Success Factors in Scrum

Each of the failure modes can be converted to a success factor, which results in a list like this:

- Prioritize having an effective Product Owner.
- Prioritize backlog refinement.
- Drive to a potentially releasable level of quality each sprint.
- Create a clear Definition of Done.
- Organize work into vertical slices.

- Keep stories small
- Limit sprints to 1–2 weeks.
- Hold daily scrums daily.
- Integrate test into the Development Team.
- Hold retrospectives every sprint.
- Apply the lessons learned from each retrospective quickly.

The person most responsible for ensuring that these success factors are present is the Scrum Master, which implies an additional success factor: *Prioritize having an effective Scrum Master.*

More details on these topics are provided in later chapters.

A Successful Sprint

A successful sprint will support the main goal of Scrum, which is to deliver a product of the highest possible value. At the sprint level, this includes:

- The sprint delivers a usable, valuable increment of the product that fully meets the Definition of Done.
- The sprint's increment (aggregate functionality) increases in value compared to the previous sprint.
- The Scrum team improves its process when compared to the previous sprint.
- The Scrum team's motivation is as good or better than it was at the end of the last sprint.

Time Allocation for a Typical Sprint

The discussion in this chapter has focused on the full range of activities that occur in Scrum, and it would be easy to conclude that not very much software development occurs in Scrum. Table 5-1 shows a representative example of how effort is allocated for developers on a Scrum team.

In the table, "ideal hours" refers to the number of project-focused hours (what's available after corporate overhead). Ideal hours of 5–6 hours per day is typical for a large, established company. Small companies can average 6–7 hours, and start-up companies sometimes average more than that.

Of the 60 ideal hours available per sprint, about 20% go into planning and process improvement and about 80% is available for development work.

Table 5-1 Example Effort Allocation During a Sprint

Sprint Planning Parameters		**Hours**
Sprint duration (business days)		10
Ideal hours per day (project-focused hours)	×	6
Total ideal hours, per developer, per sprint	=	60
Scrum Activities, per sprint, per developer		
Product backlog refinement (5%)		3
Sprint planning		4
Sprint review		2
Sprint retrospective		2
Development work		49

A Scrum Scorecard

For the sake of assessing fidelity of Scrum implementations, we have found it useful to score Scrum projects on the most important Scrum success factors. Figure 5-6 shows an example of a Scrum project star diagram.

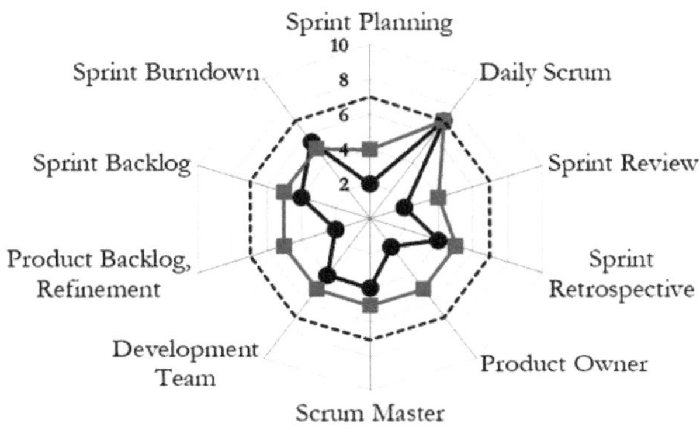

Figure 5-6
A diagnostic tool that shows a Scrum project's performance according to key Scrum success factors.

The diagram uses this key:

0	Not Used
2	Used, but with major gaps
4	Used, but with gaps
7	Used effectively
10	Optimized

The darker gray line reflects the average practice that my company has seen. The lighter gray line shows a hypothetical specific project. The dashed line shows a healthy project. As I mentioned earlier, the average Scrum project we see is not making very good use of Scrum! A healthy, effective Scrum project will have scores of 7 or higher for all of the success factors.

Why Start with Scrum?

The primary challenge in the software industry for the 35 years I've been working in it, and probably longer, has been avoiding code-and-fix development. In the 1980s and 1990s, developers would say they were doing structured programming, but many were really doing code-and-fix and missing all the benefits of structured programming. In the 1990s and 2000s, developers would say they were doing object-oriented programming, but many were still doing code-and-fix and suffering the consequences. In the 2000s and 2010s, developers and teams are saying they're doing Agile development, but even with decades of history to warn them, many are still doing code-and-fix. The more things change, the more they stay the same!

A challenge created by Agile development is that it is explicitly code-focused, which makes it more difficult to tell whether teams are using Agile development practices effectively or are doing code-and-fix. Sticky notes on the wall don't necessarily mean a team is taking an organized, effective approach to its project. Where Sequential approaches fail in bureaucracy, Agile approaches fail in anarchy.

One part of the mission of more effective Agile is ensuring that teams are actually using Agile practices—not just using Agile cosmetics as a cover for code-and-fix.

Scrum is a good place to start. If the team is following the key Scrum practices described in this chapter and the Scrum Master is coaching the team effectively, it will have a hard time devolving into code-and-fix.

Other Considerations

One hallmark of Agile development has been a proliferation of named practices. Each practice was invented for a reason, by an intelligent consultant or practitioner, and each of these practices have worked well at least one time, in at least one organization. Each of these practices has its advocates.

The focus of this book is on proven practices that have worked broadly for many organizations. The "Other Considerations" sections from this point forward in the book will describe selected practices that you might have heard of but that in my company's experience do not rise to the level of proven, broadly applicable practices.

Extreme Programming

Much of the initial focus of Agile development was on Extreme Programming (Beck, 2000) (Beck, 2005). Early attention was, as advertised, extreme, but longer-term use did not pan out. At a time when XP version 1 was described as requiring use of all 12 practices, even the projects touted as exemplar projects did not actually use all of the practices (Grenning, 2001) (Schuh, 2001) (Poole, 2001). Even the author of the foreword to the 2nd edition of *Extreme Programming Explained* professed that his teams had not fully adopted XP. Although teams today commonly refer to themselves as using Extreme Programming within a Scrum wrapper, current usage has settled into using a small number of selected XP practices (Bernstein, 2015). The bottom line is that XP has been a useful source of Agile practices but is not as useful as Scrum for beginning Agile development.

Kanban

Kanban is both less prescriptive than Scrum and less team oriented. Kanban can be more appropriate than Scrum for small teams (1–4 people) or for work that is more production oriented than project oriented.

Scrum teams often evolve toward increasing use of Kanban over time, and some organizations have had success with using Kanban as a larger-scale project portfolio management tool. But, again, Scrum is usually the most useful place to begin Agile development.

Suggested Leadership Actions

Inspect

- Interview your teams about their use of Scrum. Have them score themselves according to the Scrum scorecard. To what degree are they truly using Scrum?
- Review staffing for the Scrum Master role on your teams. Are your Scrum Masters effective at helping your teams execute Scrum practices, including the high-discipline practices associated with Scrum's failure modes?
- Review staffing for the Product Owner role on your teams. How effective are the people you have in these critical roles? Are they adding to the teams' effectiveness, or are they weak links in the chain?

Adapt

- Insist that your teams use by-the-book Scrum—unless they can show you a quantitative, measured basis for doing something different. (Chapter 21, "More Effective Agile Process Improvement," will go into more detail about measuring Agile process changes.)
- If your Scrum Masters are not effective, develop them or replace them.
- If your Product Owners are not effective, develop them or replace them.

Additional Resources

This chapter is not intended to be a complete tutorial on Scrum. Numerous good books and white papers are available on the topic, including these:

Schwaber, Ken and Jeff Sutherland. 2017. *The Scrum Guide: The Definitive Guide to Scrum: The Rules of the Game.* 2017. This is considered by many to be the definitive description of Scrum.

Rubin, Kenneth, 2012. *Essential Scrum: A Practical Guide to the Most Popular Agile Process*, Addison-Wesley, 2012. This is a comprehensive guide to Scrum that addresses common issues related to Scrum adoptions that are not part of Scrum per se.

Lacey, Mitch, 2016. *The Scrum Field Guide: Agile Advice for Your First Year and Beyond, 2d Ed.* Addison-Wesley, 2016. This is a guide to implementing Scrum that focuses on nuts and bolts practical issues that arise in Scrum implementations.

Cohn, Mike. 2010. *Succeeding with Agile: Software Development Using Scrum.* Upper Saddle River, New Jersey : Addison-Wesley, 2010. This is another good alternative to (Rubin 2012) or (Lacey 2016).

Stuart, Jenny, et al. "Six Things Every Software Executive Should Know about Scrum." Construx White Paper, July 2018.

Stuart, Jenny, et al. "Staffing Scrum Roles," Construx White Paper, August 2017.

Stuart, Jenny, et al. "Ten Keys to Successful Scrum Adoption," Construx White Paper, July 2018.

Sutherland, Jeff, 2014. *Scrum: The Art of Doing Twice the Work in Half the Time*. Crown Business: New York, 2014. This business-oriented book presents a detailed introduction to Scrum by one of the co-creators of Scrum.

CHAPTER SIX

More Effective Agile Teams

The fundamental unit of productivity in Agile development is the team—not high-performing individuals but high-performing teams. This is a key concept, and we have seen many organizations sabotage their Agile adoptions from the outset by not understanding what is needed for Agile teams to succeed and not supporting them in the ways they need to be supported.

The effective Agile team is not much different from the Microsoft cross-functional "Feature Team" popularized 20 years ago (Cusumano, 1995).

Key Principle: Build Cross-Functional Teams

An effective Agile team includes the functions or disciplines needed to work independently. An effective Agile team must be able to make decisions on its own about the vast majority of its work, including decisions about product details (requirements), technical details, and process details. The bulk of people writing production code should also be creating the bulk of automated test code and sorting out requirements details.

This normally requires at least the following specializations:

- Developers from different layers of the application (front end, back end, etc.) and with different expertise (user experience, security, etc.)
- Testers from different layers of the application
- Technical writers
- Experts in the development process being used (Scrum Master)
- Subject matter experts
- Business experts who bring business focus, vision, and ROI to the team (Product Owner)

These descriptions are roles, and multiple roles can be played by the same person. For example, developers might also be writing acceptance tests.

A high-functioning cross-functional team must have both the *ability* and the *authority* to make binding decisions in a timely way.

Ability to Make Decisions

The ability to make decisions comes from how the team is composed. Does the team include all the expertise needed to make effective decisions? Does it include expertise in architecture, quality, usability, the product, the customer, and the business—or does it have to go outside the team to find expertise in these areas?

A team that is lacking any of these areas of expertise will not have the ability to be an effective cross-functional team. The team will often encounter areas in which it does not have the expertise to make a decision. It will then need to reach out to other parts of the organization to access that expertise. This inserts numerous delays. The team will not always know whom to reach out to, and it will take time to identify the right person. The outside person will not always be available immediately. It will take time to describe the team's context to that person. If the team needs feedback on its interpretation of the outside person's input, that feedback might be subject to many of the same delays. Both the team and the outside person will make assumptions, and some of those assumptions will turn out to be mistaken, and those mistakes will take still more time to correct.

Every team will have to reach outside itself occasionally, but a team that includes all the expertise needed to make most decisions locally can close issues in minutes that would take days if the expertise is not within the team. The goal should be to set up the team so that it can close as many issues as possible on its own.

If your organization is not willing to staff your Agile teams with the expertise needed to make the vast majority of decisions locally, you'll have a high chance of failure in your Agile adoption.

Authority to Make Decisions

The authority to make decisions comes partly from having all key stakeholders represented on the team and partly from having appropriate permission from the organization. For the team to be effective, it needs the ability to make *binding decisions*—decisions that cannot be undone by others in the organization.

The absence of adequate authority gives rise to several dynamics, all of them counterproductive:

- The team will spend too much time reworking decisions that have been overturned by others in the organization.
- The team will operate at an overly deliberate pace caused by constantly looking over its shoulder in anticipation of having its decisions second-guessed or overturned.
- The team will insert wait states as it seeks approval for decisions from others in the organization.

Authority and ability must be considered as a pair. It is not effective for an organization to grant authority to make decisions if it does not also create the circumstances that give the team the ability to make decisions. If all stakeholder interests are truly represented within the team, any decision will be considered from all relevant points of view. This doesn't mean the team will never make any mistakes. It means the team will have a sound basis for making the decisions it makes and the rest of the organization will have a sound basis for trusting the team's decisions.

An organizational unwillingness to delegate the authority to make binding decisions to the team is another kiss of death for Agile teams and Agile implementations.

The Role of Mistakes

Like any other kinds of team, self-managed Agile teams will make mistakes. That will be OK if the organization has established an effective learning culture. For one thing, the team will learn from its mistakes and improve. For another, knowing that the organization trusts the team enough to let them make mistakes is a powerful motivator.

Impact of Cross-Functional Teams

The *2018 Accelerate: State of DevOps* report found that, "High-performing teams are twice as likely to be developing and delivering software in a single, cross-functional team … we found that low performers were twice as likely to be developing and delivering software in separate, silo'd teams than elite performers" (DORA, 2018).

Agile Teams as Black Boxes

The Agile practice of Scrum explicitly treats the Scrum team as a "black box." If you are an organizational leader, you are allowed to see the inputs to your teams and the outputs from your teams, but you are not supposed to be very concerned with the inner workings of the teams.

The name "Scrum" itself is intended to emphasize this characteristic. Scrum is a type of play in rugby—players pack closely together to try to move the ball down the field. It isn't at all clear what any individual player is doing at any particular time; the objective is for the *team* to make progress.

Figure 6-1
A scrum in rugby. The players pack closely together and work as a team. "Managers" can't see what's going on inside.

In a software Scrum, the same idea is implemented by saying that the team takes on a defined amount of work (the sprint goal) at the beginning of each sprint. The team commits to deliver the work—no matter what—by the end of the sprint. Then, for the duration of the sprint, the team is treated as a black box—no one gets to see inside, and no one gets to put anything else into the box during the sprint. At the end of the sprint, the team delivers the functionality it committed to at the beginning of the sprint.

As I've emphasized, Scrum sprints should be short (again, 1–2 weeks) so that managers don't have to wait long to check whether a team is meeting its commitments.

This description of the team as a black box has been exaggerated a bit to make a point. Many managers will want to understand the team's work well enough to support the team by clearing roadblocks (removing impediments), supporting staff development, coaching teams through conflict resolution, addressing priority conflicts among projects, hiring new team members, streamlining organizational bureaucracy, and so on.

At a conceptual level I believe that Scrum's approach to treating teams as black boxes leads to healthier, more effective management. Managers should not be reviewing minute technical or process details. They should be focused on making sure the team has clear direction, and they should hold the team accountable for performing to that direction. They do not need to be aware of moment-to-moment decisions or mistakes in how the team is proceeding toward its goals. Being overly concerned with details is antithetical to a number of key principles, including decriminalizing mistakes and maximizing the team's autonomy. Focus instead on clearing impediments and shielding the teams from avoidable disruption during the sprint.

Key Principle: Motivate Teams Through Autonomy, Mastery, Purpose

Most productivity studies have found that productivity depends more on motivation than any other factor (Boehm, 1981). For software development work, the only kind of motivation that matters is *internal* motivation. A company is essentially renting space in people's brains, paying its employees to think about what they want them to think about. External motivation doesn't work because you can't compel someone to think about something; you can only set up the circumstances in which they will think about your problem because they want to.

In his 2009 book, *Drive*, Daniel Pink proposed a theory of internal motivation based on the factors of Autonomy, Mastery, and Purpose. Pink's motivation theory dovetails with the support that Agile teams need to be effective.

Autonomy

"Autonomy" refers to the ability to direct your own life and work—including what you do, when you do it, and who you do it with. Autonomy is related to trust. If a person believes their organization doesn't trust them to make decisions, they won't believe they have real autonomy. The work you do to create cross-functional Agile teams that have the ability and authority to make their own decisions will support your teams' sense of autonomy.

Mastery

"Mastery" refers to the desire to learn and improve. It is not the idea of reaching a defined standard of competence, but the idea of constantly getting *better*. This is especially important for technical staff. As I pointed out many years ago in my book *Rapid Development* (McConnell, 1996), the opportunity for growth has been found to be a stronger motivator for developers than advancement, recognition, salary, status, level of responsibility, and other factors that you might assume matter more. Agile's focus on learning from experience will support your team's sense of mastery.

Purpose

"Purpose" refers to understanding why what you're working on matters. What is the big picture? How is the thing you're working on bigger and more important than yourself? How does it support your company or the world at large? Agile's focus on direct contact with customers will support your team's sense of purpose.

Table 6-1 Common Practices That Support and Undermine Autonomy

How to Support Autonomy	How to Undermine
Lead by setting direction (aligning with the broader organizational vision and mission)	Leaders concern themselves with details of how the work is performed
Commit to a direction	Change direction frequently
Include all skills on the team necessary to act independently	Withhold expertise from the team that it needs in order to work independently Do not create real teams; just groups of highly matrixed individuals
Allow teams to experiment with change to their practices based on their retrospectives	Insist on predefined processes, regardless of the team's experience
Allow teams to pull work at a pace they determine for themselves	Dictate the rate at which work is pushed to the teams
Feed requirements through the agreed-upon requirements process	Push requirements directly to the team, or to individual team members
Keep high-performing teams intact; move work to people	Frequently break up and reconfigure teams; move people to work
Allow teams to make mistakes and learn from them	Criminalize mistakes and penalize teams for them

Table 6-2 Common Practices That Support and Undermine Mastery

How to Support Mastery	How to Undermine
Allow time for retrospectives	Discourage retrospectives
Encourage changes to be made each sprint	Disallow changes, or require a bulky change-approval process
Allow technical staff to explore new technology areas	Restrict technology focus to immediate business needs
Allow time for training and professional development	Focus only on short-term project goals; don't allow time for training
Support innovation days	Discourage experimentation
Support deliberate practice such as coding katas	Insist on strict task focus; do not allow time for individual improvement
Allow staff members to move into new areas	Require staff members to stay in the area in which they have the most experience

The Virtuous Combination of Autonomy, Mastery, and Purpose

Daniel Pink's research has found that a team that works on its own, understands why it's doing its work, and is steadily improving will also be highly motivated. The factors that create an effective team also create a motivated team, and in this virtuous interaction effectiveness and motivation support each other.

Table 6-3 Common Practices That Support and Undermine Purpose

How to Support Purpose	How to Undermine
Provide technical staff with regular contact with actual customers	Restrict technical staff from interacting directly with customers
Provide technical staff with frequent contact with internal business staff	"Silo" the technical teams and business staff so that they interact only rarely
Regularly communicate the big picture surrounding the team's work	Communicate the big picture only at infrequent all-company meetings
Describe the real-world impact of the team's work: "Our defibrillator saved xyz lives last year"	Insist that big picture issues are the domain of leadership, and the team doesn't have a "need to know"
Emphasize the value of high quality work to the organization	Focus only on financial benefit to the company and/or the importance of meeting short-term delivery goals

Is Your Organization Willing to Create Agile Teams?

An Agile anti-pattern is adopting Scrum without creating truly self-managed teams. If management pays lip service to self-management while continuing to direct and control the team at the detailed level, the Agile implementation will fail.

Organizations should not adopt Agile unless they are willing to, ready to, and committed to establish and support self-managed teams.

Other Considerations

Open Office Plans

A feature of some Agile adoptions has been to shift from offices or cubes to an open floor plan to support a higher level of collaboration. I do not recommend this.

Counter to expectations, a Harvard study found that open floor plans reduced face-to-face communication by about 70% compared to cubes (Jarrett, 2018). Consensus of research for several years has found that open floor plans reduce employee satisfaction, increase stress, reduce job performance, reduce creativity, damage concentration, reduce attention spans, and decrease overall motivation (Konnikova, 2014).

Some teams might prefer open floor plans, but most do not. Indeed, backlash against open floor plans has been intense (Jarrett, 2013). One recent article's headline stated, "It's Official: Open-Plan Offices Are Now the Dumbest Management Fad of All Time" (James, 2018).

In my 1996 book, *Rapid Development*, I summarized research at that time that found that the highest levels of productivity were achieved in private or semi-private (two-person) offices (McConnell, 1996). More current research indicates that that finding has not changed.

Geographically Distributed Teams

Geographic distribution creates challenges for effective teams. These are discussed in detail in Chapter 17, "More Effective Distributed Agile Teams."

Personal Interaction Skills

People's ability to work well in teams is affected by the personal interaction skills. This factor is discussed in more detail in Chapter 16, “More Effective Individuals and Interactions.”

Personal Orientations and Roles

In addition to representation of different job functions, teams tend to perform best when they have a balance of personal orientations and roles. Belbin’s Team Role Theory provides an interesting and useful way to assess the presence of roles needed on teams, including Company Worker, Chairman, Shaper, Plant, Resource Investigator, Team Worker, Monitor/Evaluator, and Completer/Finisher. Research on IT teams shows a high correlation between having a balance of team roles and team performance (Twardochleb, 2017).

Suggested Leadership Actions

Inspect

- Review the composition of your teams. Do your teams contain all the expertise needed to make the vast majority of decisions within the teams?
- Review your personal interactions with your teams. What are you personally doing that could be interpreted as second-guessing the teams or otherwise undermining their autonomy?
- Review your organization's interactions with your teams similarly to how you reviewed your own interactions.
- Review the lists in Tables 6-1, 6-2, and 6-3. How does your organization rate according to the entries in those tables?

Adapt

- Revise the composition of your teams so that each team is truly self-managed.
- Change your own actions, as needed, to provide your teams with autonomy.
- Implement other changes based on your review of Tables 6-1, 6-2, and 6-3.

Additional Resources

Pink, Daniel H. 2009. *Drive: The Surprising Truth About What Motivates Us.* New York : Riverhead Books, 2009.

Cusumano, Michael A. and Richard Selby. 1995. *Microsoft Secrets: How the World's Most Powerful Software Company Creates Technology, Shapes Markets and Manages People.* New York, NY : Touchstone, 1995.

McConnell, Steve. 1996. *Rapid Development: Taming Wild Software Schedules.* Redmond, Washington : Microsoft Press, 1996.

CHAPTER SEVEN

More Effective Agile Projects

Agile teams work on Agile projects, and understanding what an effective Agile project looks like is just as important as understanding what's required for an effective Agile team.

The primary way software development work is organized is into projects (as opposed to individual task assignments or collections of projects), so this chapter is especially focused on the principles that matter most at the project level. I use "project" in this chapter as a general term that could also mean "program" or "release."

Key Principle: Keep Projects Small

For the past 20 years, the most-publicized Agile successes have come from Agile use on small projects. Agile development for the first 10 years focused strongly on keeping projects small, with Scrum teams made up of 5–10 people. Whether by accident or by design, this emphasis on small projects has been important because, regardless of what type of software development a team is practicing, small projects are much easier to complete successfully than large projects.

Capers Jones has been reporting for more than 20 years that small projects succeed more readily than large projects do (Jones, 1991) (Jones, 2012). I summarized much of the research on the effect of project size in my books *Code Complete, 2nd Ed.* (McConnell, 2004) and *Software Estimation: Demystifying the Black Art* (McConnell, 2006). The Standish Group's *Chaos Manifesto 2013* found that more than 75% of small projects were successful, whereas only 10% of large projects were successful (Standish Group, 2013).

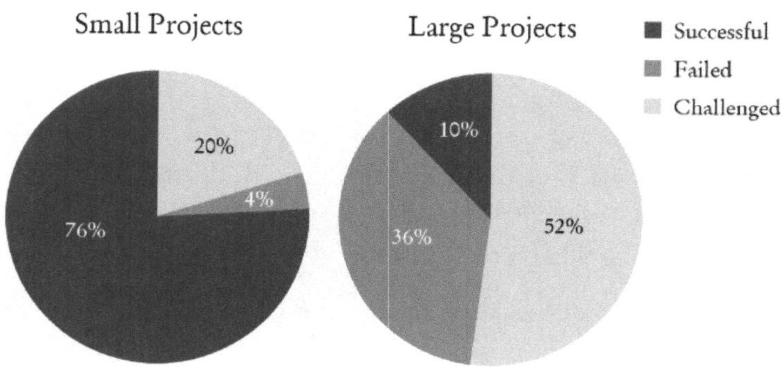

Figure 7-1

Small projects succeed much more often than large projects. The data shown is for projects from 2011.

The Standish Group also found that over a 10-year period small projects were successful far more often than large projects regardless of whether the projects used Agile or Waterfall[3] practices.

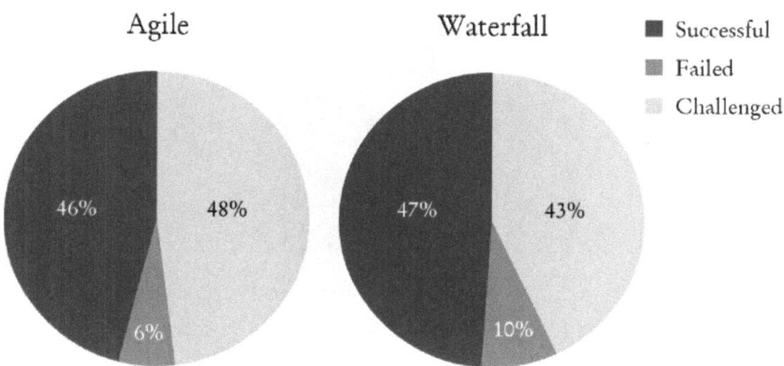

Figure 7-2
Small project success rate is virtually identical whether the project is an Agile project or a Waterfall project. The data shown is for projects from 2003 to 2012.

Because small projects are easier than large projects, the larger the project, the lower the chance of on-time or earlier delivery.

---

[3] As discussed in Chapter 1, these projects are not true Waterfall projects and would be more accurately described by what I refer to as Sequential.

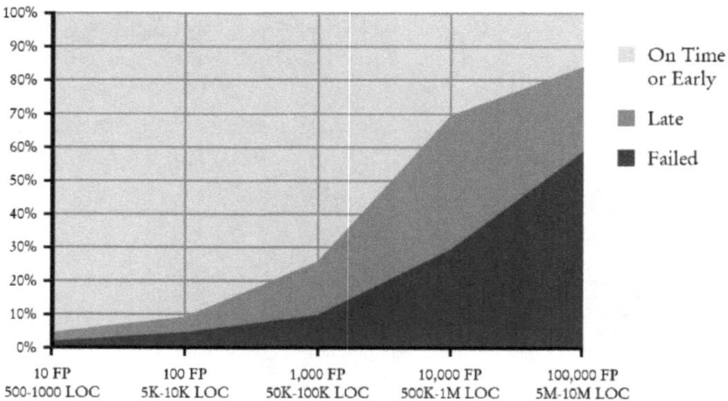

Figure 7-3

The larger the project, the lower the odds of on-time and on-budget delivery (Jones, 2012). "FP" refers to size in function points. "LOC" refers to lines of code. Comparisons of sizes in function points to sizes in lines of code are approximate.

The reasons for small projects being more successful are manifold. In general terms, larger projects involve more people on the project teams. The interconnections among people on the teams or among different teams become more complex. As the complexity of interaction increases, communication mistakes increase. Communication mistakes lead to errors in requirements, errors in design, errors in coding—in general, they lead to errors!

Furthermore, the larger the project becomes, the higher the error *rate* becomes. This is not saying merely that the total number of errors increases—larger projects produce disproportionately more errors.

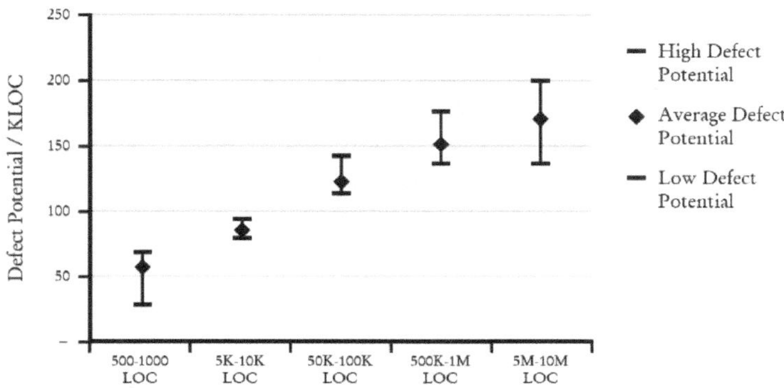

Figure 7-4

The larger the project, the larger the error rate (defect potential) is. Adapted from (Jones, 2012). LOC refers to lines of code.

As error rates and total errors go up, the effectiveness of defect removal strategies goes *down*. This means that defects remaining in the software increase disproportionately, even when considering the disproportionate increase in error rates.

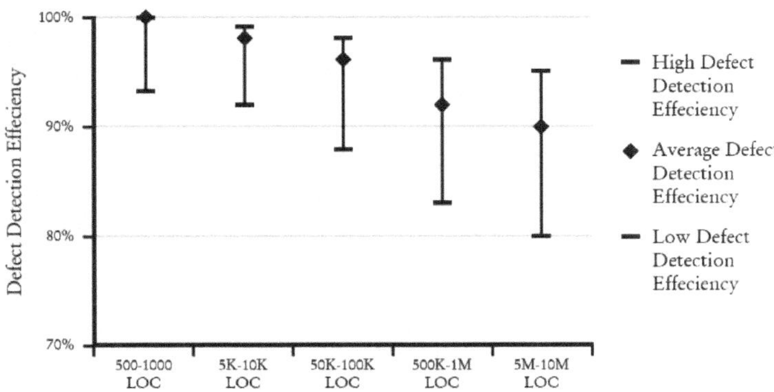

Figure 7-5

The larger the project, the less effective defect detection practices are. Adapted from (Jones, 2012).

As error rates go up, effort needed to fix the errors also goes up because a high percentage of most software projects' total effort goes into error corrections. Consequently, smaller projects have the highest per-person productivity and productivity declines as project size increases.

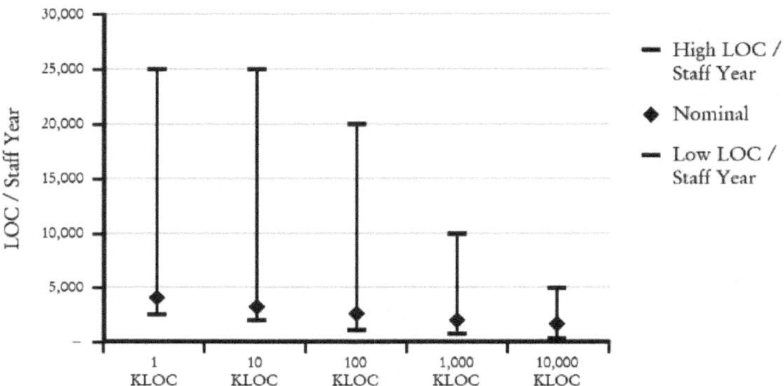

Figure 7-6

The smaller the project, the higher the per-person productivity is. Adapted from (McConnell, 2006).

The inverse relationship between size and productivity has been extensively researched and verified for more than 40 years. Fred Brooks discussed software's "diseconomy of scale" in the first edition of *The Mythical Man-Month* (Brooks, 1975). Larry Putnam's work on software estimation validated Brooks's observations about diseconomy of scale (Putnam, 1992). The Constructive Cost Model (Cocomo) estimation-related research confirmed the diseconomy of scale empirically, both in Cocomo's original research in the late 1970s and in the more rigorous, updated research in the late 1990s (Boehm, 1981) (Boehm, 2000).

The bottom line: To maximize the chances of a successful Agile project (or any kind of project), *keep the project as small as possible.*

It isn't possible, of course, to decree that every project be small rather than large. You'll find approaches to large projects (including suggestions for how to make them more like small projects) in Chapter 8, "More Effective Large Agile Projects."

Key Principle: Keep Sprints Short

A corollary to keeping projects small is keeping sprints short. You might think that the small project is good enough on its own. But short sprints of 1–2 weeks support successful projects in numerous ways, as described in the next few sections.

Short Sprints Reduce Midstream Requirements Changes

In Scrum, requirements changes are allowed to be made between sprints, but once a sprint has started, requirements cannot be added to the sprint until the next sprint. This is reasonable when sprints are only 1–2 weeks long.

If development cycles are longer, pressure to change requirements increases and it becomes less reasonable to ask stakeholders to defer their requirements requests. If a Sequential development cycle is 6 months long, asking a stakeholder to delay implementation of their requirement change until the next cycle means holding it until the beginning of the next cycle, adding it at that point, and then waiting for delivery until the end of the next cycle. That would be an average of 1.5 cycles, or 9 months.

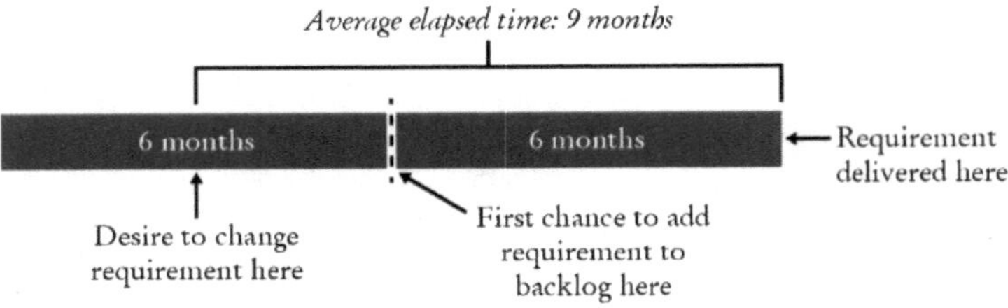

Figure 7-7
In Sequential development, if requirements cannot be changed mid-cycle, the wait time to change a requirement and have it be delivered can be lengthy.

In contrast, Scrum's typical 2-week sprints means that the stakeholder who wants a requirement change needs to wait an average of only 3 weeks for the change.

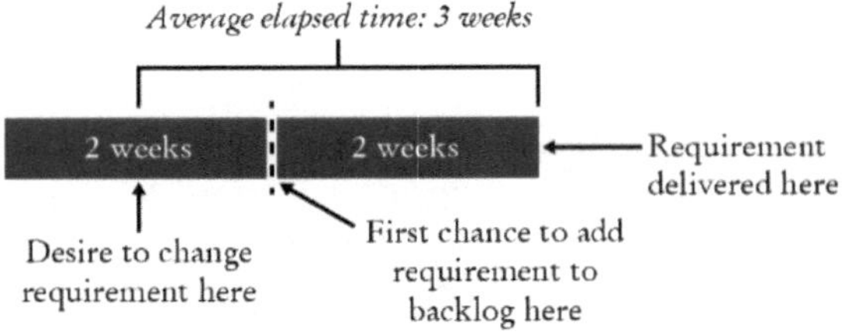

Figure 7-8
Shorter development cycles provide much more frequent opportunities to make requirements changes.

Asking a stakeholder to wait 9 months for their change to be delivered is often not reasonable. Asking the stakeholder to wait 3 weeks is virtually always reasonable, which means Scrum teams can work with much less fear of mid-sprint requirements changes.

Short Sprints Support More Responsiveness to Customers and Stakeholders

Every sprint provides a new opportunity to demonstrate working software and incorporate stakeholder feedback. It also provides an opportunity to accept requirements changes, incorporate them into the overall product backlog, and plan them into upcoming sprint backlogs. Longer sprints provide fewer opportunities for this to happen. In Scrum's typical 2-week sprints, teams give themselves 26 opportunities per year to be responsive! With a 3-month development cycle, they give themselves only four opportunities. Fifteen years ago, a 3-month schedule would have been considered a short project, but such a schedule today means you are missing opportunities to be more responsive to your stakeholders, customers, and the market.

Short Sprints Support Rapid Improvement Through Frequent Inspect and Adapt Cycles

The more often a team iterates, the more opportunities it gives itself to reflect on its experiences, learn from them, and incorporate learnings into its work practices. The same reasoning about frequency that applied to customer responsiveness applies in this area: Would you rather give your teams a chance to Inspect and Adapt—and improve—26 times each year or only four times each year? The improvement cycle made possible by short sprints helps your team improve more quickly.

Short Sprints Expose Cost and Schedule Risks

Short sprints also provide frequent opportunities to check the progress of the project. Within just a few sprints on a new project, the team will demonstrate its "velocity," or rate of progress. Based on observed progress, it becomes easy to forecast how long the overall release will take. If the project is going to take longer than originally planned, that will become evident only a few weeks into the project—a powerful realization made possible by the sprints' short duration.

Short Sprints Increase Team Accountability

When a team is responsible for delivering working functionality every 2 weeks, there is no opportunity for the team to "go dark" for extended periods. They bring their work out in public for the sprint review meetings and demonstrate it to stakeholders every couple of weeks—more often to the Product Owner. Work is accepted by the Product Owner or not, and progress becomes easy to see.

Short Sprints Increase Individual Accountability

For generations, software teams have suffered from *prima donna* developers who go off to work in a dark room for months at a time with no signs of progress. This is no longer an issue with Scrum. The necessity of standing up each day and describing what was accomplished the day before—combined with the peer pressure of supporting the team's goals for the sprint—does not allow that kind of behavior. Either the *prima donna* starts to cooperate, which resolves the issue one way, or the *prima donna* can't stand the pressure and leaves the team, which resolves the issue another way. In my opinion, either outcome is better than having a developer work unaccountably for weeks or months at a time.

Short Sprints Offer a Frequent Sense of Accomplishment

A team that delivers working software every 2 weeks feels a great, frequently recurring sense of accomplishment and has opportunities to celebrate its achievements. This contributes to a sense of mastery, which increases motivation.

The overall value of short sprints can be summarized as, "Speed of delivery beats scope of delivery in all respects." Delivering small amounts of functionality on a frequent cadence provides numerous benefits compared to delivering large amounts of functionality on an infrequent cadence.

Key Principle: Use Velocity-Based Planning

Velocity-based planning and tracking using story points is not part of textbook Scrum, but in my experience it should be. Story points should be used in four ways.

Sizing the Product Backlog

Story point estimation is used to size the product backlog. This is done early in a release cycle and as work is added to or removed from the backlog.

Calculating Velocity

The amount of work the team commits to each sprint is counted using story points. The number of story points the team delivers each sprint becomes the team's "velocity." Velocity is calculated on a sprint-by-sprint basis, and average velocity is also calculated.

Sprint Planning

The team uses story points as the basis for planning how much work it can commit to in a sprint, based on the team's observed velocity. If a team has been averaging 20 story points per sprint, and the team's proposed sprint goal would require the team to complete 40 story points, the team should scale back its plans. If one of the team members is going on vacation or if several teams members will be attending training, the team might commit to fewer story points for that sprint than it has been averaging. If the average of 20 story points has been accomplished through many late nights and weekends and is not sustainable, the team should plan for a lower number. If the team has been accomplishing its sprint goals comfortably and the team's sense is that its sprint goal of 25 story points is a "soft 25," it might commit to a higher number than its average velocity. In all cases, the team uses its average velocity as a reality check for its sprint planning.

Release Tracking

The average velocity can be used to estimate or forecast how much time is needed to complete the work in the product backlog. If the product backlog consists of 200 story points and the team has a velocity of 20 story points per sprint, it should take the team about 10 sprints to complete the work in the backlog.

Key Principle: Deliver in Vertical Slices

For short sprints to work, teams need to develop the capability to deliver small chunks of working functionality on a frequent basis. The design approach used to support this is called "vertical slicing." Some teams lack the design skill to do this and will need to develop it.

The concept of vertical slicing refers to making the changes in each architectural layer that needs to be changed to deliver the incremental functionality or value.

A vertical slice represents full stack functionality, such as "Add this field to a bank statement" or "Provide confirmation of the transaction to the user one second faster." Each of these examples would typically require work throughout the technology stack.

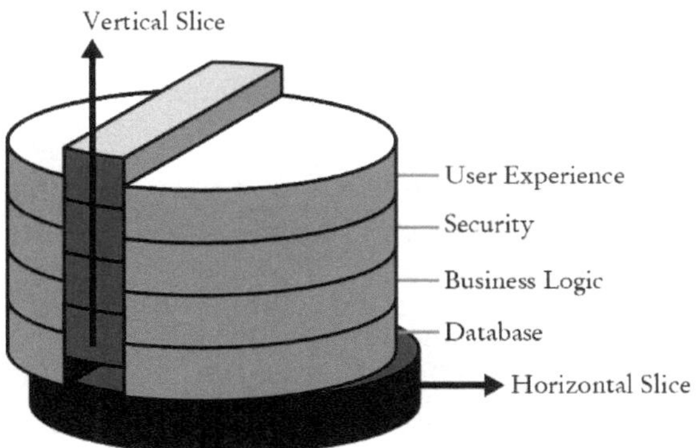

Figure 7-9
Horizontal and vertical slicing. Vertical slicing includes work in all the architectural layers needed to deliver incremental functionality.

Teams will sometimes object to vertical slicing, typically on the basis of efficiency. They will argue that it's more efficient to complete a larger chunk of work at the business logic layer before moving to the UX layer, for example. This approach is called "horizontal slicing."

It might be true that in some cases a certain technical efficiency is gained from working in horizontal slices. But that technical efficiency tends to be a sub-optimization that's outweighed by larger value-delivery considerations. And contrary to the claims that horizontal slicing leads to increased efficiency, my company has found that many teams experience significant rework arising from delivering in horizontal slices.

Vertical Slices Support Tighter Project Feedback Loops

Vertical slicing puts functionality in front of business users sooner, which supports earlier feedback on the correctness of the functionality.

Because it requires end-to-end development, vertical slicing forces the team to work through its design assumptions and implementation assumptions collaboratively, which provides useful top-to-bottom technical feedback to the team.

And vertical slicing supports end-to-end testing, which tightens the testing feedback loop.

Vertical Slices Support Delivery of Higher Business Value

Vertical slices are easier for nontechnical business stakeholders to understand, which increases the quality of business decision making about the priority and sequencing of different functionality.

Because vertical slices offer complete increments of functionality, they also provide the opportunity to put working functionality into users' hands more often, which also increases business value.

What Teams Need to Implement Vertical Slicing

Delivering in vertical slices depends both on team composition and on specific design skills. Team composition requires cross-functional, cross-discipline teams. Teams need to include business, development, and testing capability, and they need to include the skills to develop across the full technology stack.

Teams might also need to shift their design and implementation thinking to think in terms of vertical slices rather than components or horizontal-layer work.

Finally, teams need to be fed work in vertical slices. The Product Owner and the team must approach backlog refinement in a way that produces vertical slices.

Key Principle: Develop a Growth Mindset

The idea of "more effective" Agile is a constantly moving target. No matter how effective you are this year, you can be more effective next year. For this to take place, however, teams must be allowed to spend time improving. Some of that improvement should happen in the regular cycle of sprint retrospectives and sprint planning, and some improvement should occur during the sprints.

Becoming more effective requires a growth mindset—a mindset of "we can get better over time"—which not all leaders have.

Some software leaders look at software projects as having the kinds of inputs and outputs shown in Figure 7-10. In this view, the only relevant output from a software project is the software itself.

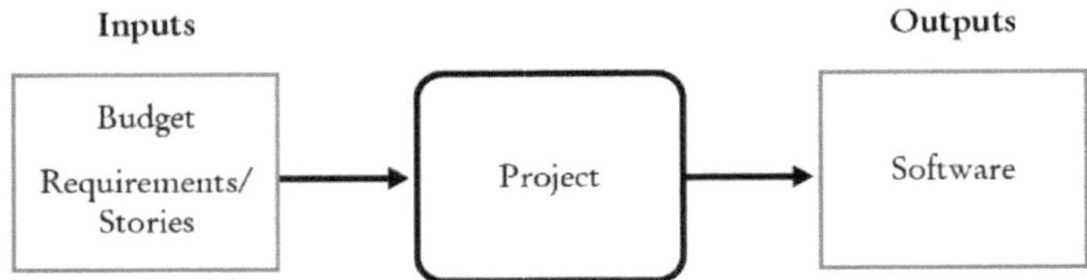

Figure 7-10

A simplistic view of the inputs and outputs to a software project.

A more holistic view of a project's inputs and outputs considers the capability of the team before and after the project. A project that's exclusively task-focused—which usually includes a dose of schedule pressure—can produce inputs and outputs like those shown in Figure 7-11.

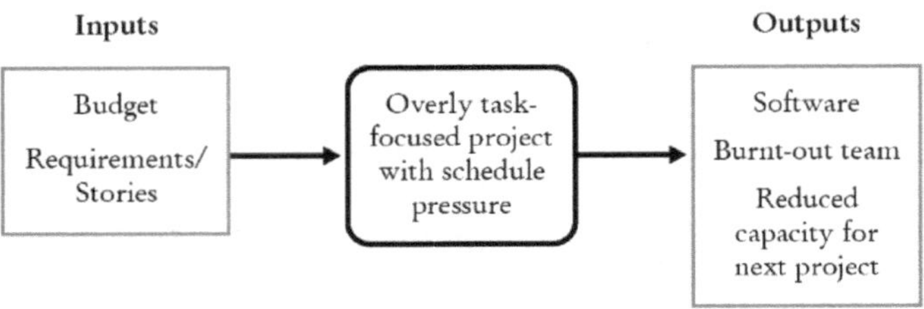

Figure 7-11

Inputs and outputs for a software project that takes a narrow view of the project's purpose.

If the leader isn't focused on growing the team, it's easy to run a project in a way that produces a worn-out team that has *less capacity* than the team had at the beginning of the project. The same logic applies to sprints and releases. Some Scrum teams experience "sprint fatigue" when sprints are not run at a sustainable pace.

The delta between how teams start their projects and how they end their projects significantly influences the effectiveness of the organization. In many organizations, every project is a rush project. Projects focus exclusively on the tasks immediately in front of them, and there's never time for the individuals or teams to get better at what they do. Indeed, constant schedule pressure literally makes them worse at what they do—in terms of their feelings of autonomy, mastery, and, ultimately, motivation.

This leads to a predictable set of dynamics in which teams experience burnout, the best team members leave for other organizations, and organizational capacity degrades over time.

An organization committed to being more effective will take a more comprehensive, growth-mindset view of the purpose of its software projects. Of course, one purpose of the project is to produce working software, but another purpose is enhancing the capabilities of the team that produces the software: *"We can get better over time, and we will allow time to do that."*

A growth mindset produces several benefits to the organization:

- Increased individual energy level
- Improved individual and team motivation
- Higher team cohesion
- Increased company loyalty (better retention)
- Expanded technical and nontechnical skill sets

Indeed, a 2019 survey by McKinsey & Company and Scrum.org found that the #1 intrinsic characteristic of an Agile practitioner was *growth mindset* (Aghina, 2019).

A company that realizes how much benefit a growth mindset makes possible will conduct its projects as shown in 7-12.

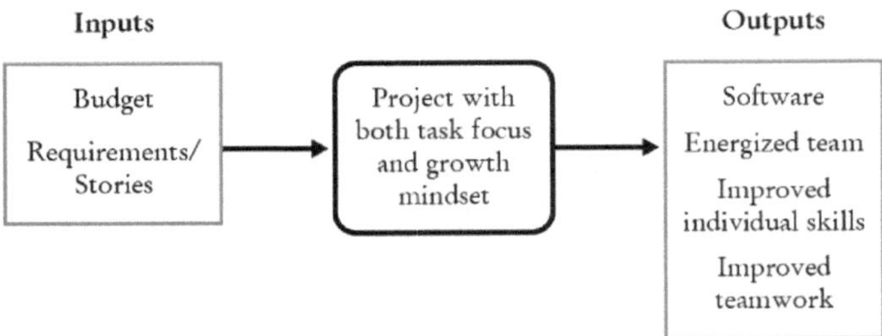

Figure 7-12
Inputs and outputs for a software project that takes a wider and long-term view of the project's purpose.

The traditional Agile mantra of "sustainable pace" is one necessary element of more effective Agile, but that implies merely that teams won't burn out, not that they will continually get better. A commitment to a growth mindset takes the foundation established by working at a sustainable pace and leverages it to provide significant benefits to the organization.

Key Principle: Develop Business Focus

There are no silver bullets in software development, but there is a business-oriented practice that's close, and far too few organizations employ it. The practice is simple, and its benefits are greatly out of proportion with its difficulty.

What is this near-silver bullet? It is simply putting every single developer in direct contact with actual customers, with actual users of their system.

Some businesses resist putting developers in contact with customers because they fear that the great unwashed masses of developers are, well, literally unwashed. They treat the Product Owner (or Sales, or Business Analyst) as a shield between developers and customers. This is a mistake and a significant lost opportunity.

For a developer, experiencing direct contact with customers is often a life-changing experience. A developer who previously argued for technical purity (whatever that is) and viewed customers mainly as an annoying source of illogical and inconsistent feature requests becomes a vigorous advocate for ease of use and customer satisfaction.

Business leaders who expose developers to real customers invariably report that the benefit their teams gain in understanding the customer perspective far outweighs any risks they were concerned about. Technical staff members develop an understanding of how their work is used in the field, how much customers depend on it, what frustrates customers, and how much impact their work can have when it's done in a way that meets their customers' needs. There is a strong interplay between exposing developers to customers and the Purpose part of Autonomy, Mastery, and Purpose. This means you not only receive product-quality benefits from this practice but also can realize a motivation benefit.

Here are ways you can expose developers to customers:

- Have a developer listen to support calls for a few hours at a time, periodically.
- Have a developer field support calls for a week.
- Send a developer to customer sites to observe customers using their software.
- Have developers observe users in a UX lab through a one-way glass or TV monitor.
- Have a developer accompany sales staff on customer visits.

These practices are not treated as rewards or penalties but as part of maintaining a healthy business.

Putting developers in direct contact with customers is an incredibly simple idea that is practiced far too seldom, yet it yields significant results whenever it's done.

Other Considerations

Not all software development work occurs in projects. Ad hoc software work is common in handling support tickets, production issues, patches, and so on.

This kind of work certainly qualifies as software development work, and it is also amenable to Agile practices. It can made more efficient, higher quality, and more methodical through adoption of Agile practices such as Lean and Kanban. However, in my experience, organizations tend to struggle with this kind of work much less than they struggle with project-size software development work, so this book focuses on projects rather than ad hoc work streams.

If you have a significant amount of non-project software development work in your organization, the "Additional Resources" section provides some resources on that topic.

Sustainable Pace

The Agile notion of "sustainable pace" rephrased an original notion of 40-hour work week. Most Agile writing today interprets sustainable pace as "no evenings or weekends, ever." I think this is simplistic and ignores differences in individuals' work preferences. A steady 40 hours per week amounts to a sustainable pace for some people, but for others that amounts to a recipe for boredom. I personally have done much of my best work in burst mode—55 hours for a couple weeks, and then 30 hours for a couple weeks after that. The average might work out to about 40 hours per week, but individual weeks aren't very close to 40 hours.

The details that make up "sustainable pace" are not the same for everyone.

Suggested Leadership Actions

Inspect

- Review your organization's history of project outcomes. Does your organization's experience match the general pattern that small projects are successful more often than large projects?
- Review your project portfolio. Which of your large projects could be broken into multiple small projects?
- Review your teams' cadences. Are their sprints no more than 2 weeks long?
- Investigate whether your teams are using velocity-based planning.
- Have your teams score their own motivation and morale at the beginning and end of each project or release cycle. Do the numbers show that the teams are working at a sustainable pace, or are they burning out?

Adapt

- Create a plan to ensure that your teams are healthier at the ends of their projects and have developed more capabilities than they had at the beginnings.
- Insist that your teams consider their velocity when establishing their sprint goals.
- Communicate to your teams that you want them to spend a little bit of time learning each cycle. If your organization has a history of schedule pressure, communicate the focus on learning at least once a week for at least one quarter.
- Create a plan to put your technical staff into direct contact with your customers.

Additional Resources

Many of the suggestions in this chapter come directly from my company's experience in working with software organizations. As a result, additional reading on these topics is limited.

Brooks, Fred. 1975. *Mythical Man-Month.* Reading, Massachusetts : Addison-Wesley, 1975. Although dated at this point, this book contains the original classic discussion of the challenges of succeeding on large projects.

McConnell, Steve. 2019. Understanding Software Projects Lecture Series. *Construx OnDemand.* [Online] 2019. https://ondemand.construx.com. These lectures extensively discuss software project dynamics related to project size.

Standish Group. 2013. *Chaos Manifesto 2013: Think Big, Act Small.* 2013.

Rubin, Kenneth, 2012. *Essential Scrum: A Practical Guide to the Most Popular Agile Process*, Addison-Wesley, 2012. This comprehensive guide to Scrum describes use of story points and velocity for sprint planning and release planning.

CHAPTER EIGHT

More Effective Large Agile Projects

The naturalist Stephen Jay Gould tells a story in which two girls are talking on the playground (Gould, 1977). One girl says, "What if a spider was as big as an elephant? Wouldn't that be scary?" The other girl responds, "No. If a spider was as big as an elephant, it would look like an elephant, silly."

Gould goes on to explain that the second girl is right because the sizes of the organisms significantly dictate what the organisms look like. At the size of a spider, surface tension is a stronger force than gravity. So the spider can have an exoskeleton and skinny legs that allow it to crawl upside down across a ceiling. At the size of an elephant, surface tension isn't a consideration, but gravity matters a lot. Exoskeletons are not workable at that size, and an elephant must have thick legs to allow it to stand upright against the force of gravity. Gould concludes that if a spider was as a big as an elephant, it would look more like an elephant, because at that size it really has to.

For us, the analogous question for software projects is, "What if an Agile project was really large? Wouldn't that be scary?" Well, maybe it wouldn't be scary, but a line of reasoning similar to the elephant and spider analysis applies.

What's Really Different About Agile—On Large Projects?

In my judgment, the question of how to be effective on large Agile projects is not really the right question. The fact is that organizations have struggled with large projects since the beginning of software (Brooks, 1975). They have also struggled with small projects. Agile practices and Scrum in particular have allowed small projects to be successful more often, and that has shifted the focus to the large projects that still struggle.

One key to understanding how to be more successful with large *Agile* projects to understand what's needed to succeed with large projects *in general.* The "Additional Resources" section at the end of this chapter points to resources in that area.

The rest of this chapter focuses on large-project issues unique to Agile development.

Agile Emphases on Large Projects

As I described in the beginning of the book (in the "What's Really Different About Agile?" chapter), some of the emphases in Agile development support large projects and

Table 8-1 Implications of the Agile Emphases for Large Projects

Agile Emphasis	Large Project Implication
Short release cycles	The ideal is to have large project teams with short release cycles.
End-to-end development work performed in small batches	No change; large project teams can still complete end-to-end development in small batches, albeit with a higher level of coordination required
High-level up-front planning with just-in-time detailed planning	The proportion of up-front planning will need to increase.
High-level up-front requirements with just-in-time detailed requirements	Larger projects require more requirements coordination, which implies longer lead time from beginning of refinement to completion of implementation.
Emergent design	The cost of error and redesign increases as project size increases; this is the primary factor that influences the ability to be Agile on a large project.
Continuous testing, integrated into development	This is an excellent emphasis regardless of the size of the project.
Frequent structured collaboration	This emphasis becomes even more important on large projects; the specific forms of collaboration will change.
OODA as improvement model	This emphasis works just as well on large projects as on small projects.

some are diametrically opposed. Table 8-1 summarizes how Agile emphases play into large projects.

Agile's focus on completing end-to-end development work in small batches supports effective work on large projects, as does the focus on continuous testing, frequent structured collaboration, and OODA.

Depending on the nature of the project and the project's architecture, sometimes the emphasis on short release cycles needs to be moderated and sometimes it doesn't.

Agile's emphases on just-in-time planning, just-in-time requirements, and emergent design need to be moderated to support large projects. This has implications for sprint planning, sprint reviews, product backlog structure, backlog refinement, release planning, and release burndown.

Different organizations can have radically different definitions of "large" when they refer to large projects, so it's important to keep in mind what you mean by large. We've worked with organizations in which any project that requires more than one Scrum team is considered large. We've worked with other organizations in which any project smaller than 100 people is considered medium or small.

Differences in terminology aside, the considerations in this chapter come into play any time you have more than one team involved. Depending on the number of teams involved, they come into play to different degrees, as illustrated in Figure 8-1.

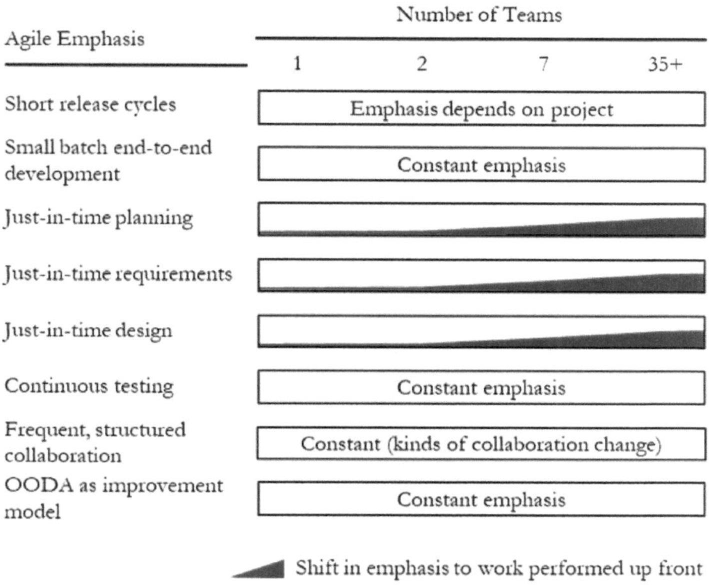

Agile Emphasis	Number of Teams: 1 — 2 — 7 — 35+
Short release cycles	Emphasis depends on project
Small batch end-to-end development	Constant emphasis
Just-in-time planning	
Just-in-time requirements	
Just-in-time design	
Continuous testing	Constant emphasis
Frequent, structured collaboration	Constant (kinds of collaboration change)
OODA as improvement model	Constant emphasis

Shift in emphasis to work performed up front

Figure 8-1
How the Agile emphases change based on project size.

The following sections describe specifics of the adaptations needed to support successful large Agile projects.

Brooks' Law

One perspective on how to infuse more effective Agile practices into a large project was prefigured by Fred Brooks in the *Mythical Man-Month* (Brooks, 1975). In the course of discussing "Brooks' Law"—the idea that adding people to a late project will make it later—Brooks makes the argument that if the work can be *completely partitioned*, Brooks' law doesn't necessarily apply.

This is directly relevant for the large project discussion because the ideal for a large project is to break it up into a set of *completely partitioned* small projects. If you can succeed in doing that, you will benefit in numerous ways. You will increase per-person productivity and reduce error rates, as described in Chapter 7, "More Effective Agile Projects." You will also open the door to emphasizing Agile practices more than Sequential practices.

As Brooks points out, however, the challenge in breaking a single large project into multiple small projects is accomplishing the goal of completely partitioning the work. If the work is only *mostly partitioned*—meaning it still requires some degree of coordination between different project teams—the multiple small projects begin to look and act more like a single large project, and you've lost what you were trying to accomplish.

Conway's Law

You can't really understand large projects and how to maximize their agility without understanding Conway's Law. The law, loosely speaking, says that the technical structure of a system reflects the structure of the human organization that built the system (Conway, 1968).[4] This structure includes the formal management structure and also the informal interpersonal network structure.

Conway's Law is a two-way street. The technical design influences the human organization design, and vice versa. If the technical design is based on a large monolithic architecture, the project team is going to struggle tremendously if it

---

[4] Conway's exact language is this: "Organizations which design systems (in the broad sense used here) are constrained to produce designs which are copies of the communication structures of these organizations."

tries to be anything other than large and monolithic. Likewise, if the team is geographically distributed across three sites but the technical architecture isn't set up to support work in three largely independent areas, the teams will again struggle because they will have technical dependencies on one anothers' work that span geographic boundaries.

Tying Conway's Law and Fred Brooks's discussions together, the implication for large Agile projects is that the ideal architecture of a large system will support *completely partitioning* the work of the teams that work on it. This ideal will be easier to achieve on some systems than others. Legacy systems, in particular, usually need to adopt some kind of crawl, walk, run approach.

Specific Architecture Suggestions

An architecture tutorial is outside the scope of this book, but the following sections contain thumbnail descriptions of architectural approaches that support small teams on large projects.

The Basics: Loose Coupling, Modularity

Strive for a loosely coupled architecture (modular and layered if possible) with readable and low-complexity code.

The architecture doesn't need to be perfectly factored microservices code. It just needs to provide enough flexibility to support the business's needs.

The holy grail that is sometimes described is to break your system into, say, 50 microservices. They can be highly modular, running in their own hosted containers with their own databases. They can each have their own versioned and authenticated APIs. They can all be released to production and scaled independently, which approaches the goal of having 50 completely partitioned development teams.

This is all a fantastic vision, and sometimes it actually works! But if some of the processing paths in your system call into numerous other parts of your system, which in turn call into numerous other parts of your system (known as "high fan out"), you can end up with significant processing overhead in the software and significant communication overhead among the teams working on the different microservices. You would probably be better off both in the software and the team structure to aggregate the system into fewer processes.

There's no one right answer for any of this, and good solutions depend on applying a combination of technical judgment about design and management judgment about the team's organization.

Avoid Monolithic Databases

Avoiding having one big database helps support partitioned teams. Loosely federated databases can support loose coupling and strong modularity within teams. But, depending on the relationships among parts of the system, it's also possible to create complex interactions that lead to significant overhead, latency, and opportunity for errors. A combination of technical judgement and team-management judgment is required to know how much to decompose a system to support loosely coupled teams while maintaining a high quality technical solution. Sometimes decomposition helps, sometimes it hurts, and sometimes it's neutral.

Use Queues

Decoupling or time shifting through the use of queues can also support loosely coupled development teams. In abstract terms, this consists of putting tasks into a queue for another part of the system to process later. The "later" could be microseconds later. The key concept in this guideline is that the system is not merely executing most of its code in an immediate, rigid, request-response loop. Using queues supports a high level of decoupling between key parts of system functionality, which allows for decoupling in the architecture and the development team (another instance of Conway's Law).

It can be useful to think about key "seams" in a system architecture. The seams represent boundaries for which, within the boundary, there is a lot of interaction but across the boundary there isn't much interaction. For the sake of loose coupling, it can be useful to uses queues for the coupling across the seams. As with the microservices description, it's possible to take this too far—50 processes managing 50 task queues with dependencies can create a different set of coupling issues, which could end up being worse than the problem the queueing is trying to solve.

Use Design by Contract

Design by contract is a design approach in which special attention is paid to interfaces. Each interface is considered to have "pre-conditions" and "post-conditions." The preconditions are the promises that the user of a component makes to the component about the conditions that will be true before the component is used. The post-conditions are the promises that the component makes back to the rest of the system about the conditions that will be true by the time the component completes its work.

Bearing Conway's Law in mind, you can use design by contract to eliminate the impact of technical dependencies on flow. The "contract" will govern the interface between parts of the software system and will implicitly set expectations for the human interfaces too.

Key Principle: Support Large Agile Projects Through Architecture

For a system's architecture to support completely partitioning the work, some architecture work must be done. Some older systems evolve toward a loosely coupled architecture, but for new systems the implication is that architecture work must be done up front to support completely partitioning the work of multiple small teams.

Some Agile teams will balk at the idea of doing "BDUF" (Big Design Up Front), under the criticism that it "isn't Agile." But as Stephen Jay Gould implied forty years ago, when you take an approach whose core emphases cluster around keeping projects small and try to make it work for projects that are large, *something* has to give. You can't change nothing and expect projects to scale successfully.

If Conway's Law is fully considered, the only factor that really needs to be modified is the emphasis on emergent design, and the planning needed to support that. A focus on up-front architecture with a goal of allowing work to be completely partitioned will support keeping teams small, which means the rest of the Agile emphases can remain. The focus on emergent design can also still remain, within the highly partitioned areas in which each small team is working.

It is not coincidence that the focus on small Agile teams has coincided over the past few years with the emergence of microservices architecture. The goal of microservices architecture is to structure an application as a set of loosely coupled services. Similarly, the goal of structuring a large Agile project is to structure the human organization as a set of loosely coupled small teams.

The organization that succeeds in architecting a large system to support completely partitioned work will not perceive itself as having a large project. It will feel like it has a collection of small teams working independently, with the only thing they have in common being that they all happen to be contributing to a common code base.

A Large Project Agile Scorecard

We have found it useful to score project performance on the main challenge areas that arise on large Agile projects. Assuming use of Scrum, Figure 8-2 shows an example of a large-project star diagram.

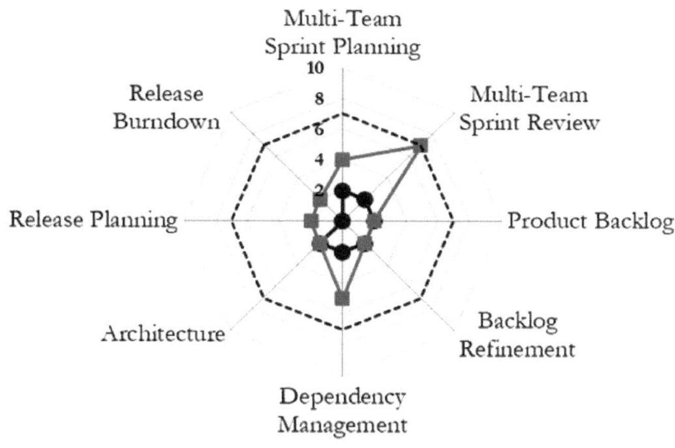

Figure 8-2

A diagnostic tool that shows large-project performance according to key large-project success factors.

The diagram uses this key:

0 Not Used
2 Used, but with major gaps
4 Used, but with gaps
7 Used effectively
10 Optimized

The darker gray line reflects the average practice that my company has seen. The lighter gray line shows a hypothetical specific project. The dashed line shows a healthy large project. To have a good chance of success, you should see scores of 7 or higher.

Other Considerations

Scaling approaches in general, not just on Agile projects, suffer from misdiagnosing the kind of coordination that needs to occur as projects scale. The larger your project becomes, the more you'll need all of the noncoding activities of requirements, architecture, configuration management, QA/Test, project management, and process. The key question is whether any one of these areas needs to scale faster or requires more coordination than the rest.

Scrum of Scrums

One reason that the Scrum of Scrums approach has had difficulty getting traction, in my view, is that it misdiagnoses the area in which large projects most commonly need additional coordination. By having Scrum Masters be the default attendees to the coordination meetings, Scrum of Scrums implies that the largest challenges will arise in the areas of process and general workflow. But experience says that the most common source of challenges for software projects is requirements. Thus, in the general case, it is more useful to have Product Owners attend the coordination meetings than Scrum Masters.

While requirements coordination support is the most common need, specific project needs vary. In my experience, large project coordination issues occur in this order of frequency:

- Requirements (most frequently)
- Architecture (on design-intensive systems)
- Configuration management
- QA/Test
- Project management
- Process

With process at the bottom of the list, Scrum of Scrum's choice for the focus of coordination work seems misguided. In contrast, SAFe structures a lot of coordination around requirements rather than around process, which is a better first-order approximation of what's needed. But there's no reason to settle for a first-order approximation. As you consider your organization's large projects, review those projects' most common sources of challenges. Then plan your coordination around that.

SAFe

SAFe is by far the most commonly used approach for large Agile projects among the companies we've worked with. The SAFe framework is well thought out, it's been steadily evolving and improving, and it has some truly useful elements. Having said that, only a few of the companies we've worked with have been satisfied with their SAFe implementations, and those have been highly customized.

The main limitation of SAFe is that is works best in organizations that have about 300 technical staff or more, which is larger than what most organizations consider to be a "large" project.

As Barry Boehm and Richard Turner wrote in *Balancing Agility and Discipline*, scaling up a process that's too small tends to work better than scaling down a process that's too large (Boehm, 2004).

Suggested Leadership Actions

Inspect

- Discuss your architecture with your key technical leaders from the perspective of Conway's Law. In what ways do you see the human organization aligning with the technical organization, and vice versa?
- Review the human organization of your largest projects. To what degree is the work truly partitioned vs. monolithic? How complex is the web of communication paths in the human organization, and how do those relate to the software architecture?
- Review the Agile emphases in Table 8-1. Consider whether there is any easier, alternate way for your organization to maintain most of the emphases in the table without relaxing the focus on emergent design.

Adapt

- Make a plan for evolving your architecture to support a more loosely coupled team structure.

Additional Resources

Conway, Melvin E. 1968. How do Committees Invent? *Datamation.* April 1968.

Gould, Stephen Jay. 1977. *Ever Since Darwin.* s.l. : WW Norton & Co Inc, 1977.

Martin, Robert C. 2017. *Clean Architecture: A Craftsman's Guide to Software Structure and Design.* s.l. : Prentice Hall, 2017.

Bass, Len, et al. 2012. *Software Architecture in Practice, 3rd Ed.* s.l. : Addison-Wesley Professional, 2012.

McConnell, Steve. 2004. *Code Complete, 2nd Ed.* Redmond, Washington : Microsoft Press, 2004. Chapter 27 describes some of the dynamics of large vs. small projects, focusing on the way that the proportion of activities change at the project level as project size changes.

McConnell, Steve. 2019. Understanding Software Projects Lecture Series. *Construx OnDemand.* [Online] 2019. https://ondemand.construx.com. Many of the lectures in this series focus on issues related to project size.

Boehm, Barry and Richard Turner. 2004. *Balancing Agility and Discipline: A Guide for the Perplexed.* Boston : Addison-Wesley, 2004. This book is a valuable source of insights into specific dynamics of project size and agility—for the expert reader. For the less expert reader the book is too mired in Agile practices circa 2004 to be useful today (main Agile focus is on XP; doesn't discuss Definition of Done' assumes long, 30 day sprints; no notion of backlog refinement, etc.).

CHAPTER NINE

More Effective Agile Quality

"If you can't find the time to do it right, where will you find the time to do it over?" has been a mantra in quality-focused organizations for generations. The means used to achieve this objective have steadily evolved, and modern Agile development has contributed some useful practices.

Key Principle: Minimize the Defect Detection Gap

We don't usually think of it this way, but defect creation is a constant on software projects. For every hour the development team works, some number of defects are created. Thus, the cumulative defect-insertion line on a software project is essentially the same as the cumulative effort line.

In contrast with the defect insertion, defect detection and removal is not a function of general effort. It is a function of a specific kind of effort: quality assurance (QA) activities.

As Figure 9-1 illustrates, on many projects defect detection and removal significantly lags defect insertion. This is problematic because the area between the two lines represents latent defects—defects that have been inserted into the software but haven't been detected and removed yet. Each of those defects represents extra bug-fixing work that is rarely "on plan." Each of those defects represents work that will unpredictably extend the budget, extend the schedule, and, in general, disrupt the project.

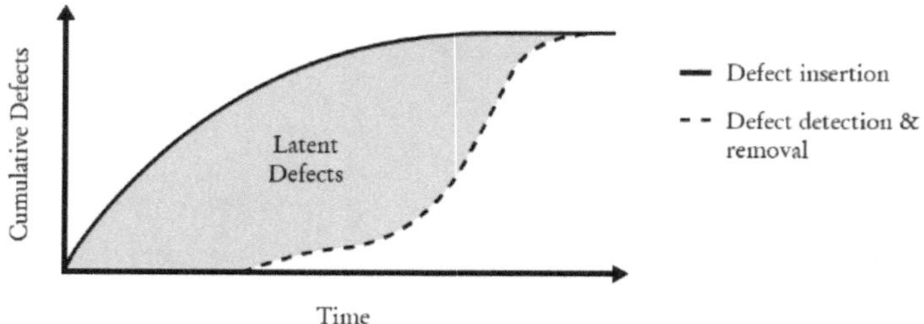

Figure 9-1
The gap between the cumulative defect-insertion line and the defect-detection-and-removal line represents latent defects.

Well-run projects attempt to minimize the gap between defect insertion and defect detection, as shown in Figure 9-2.

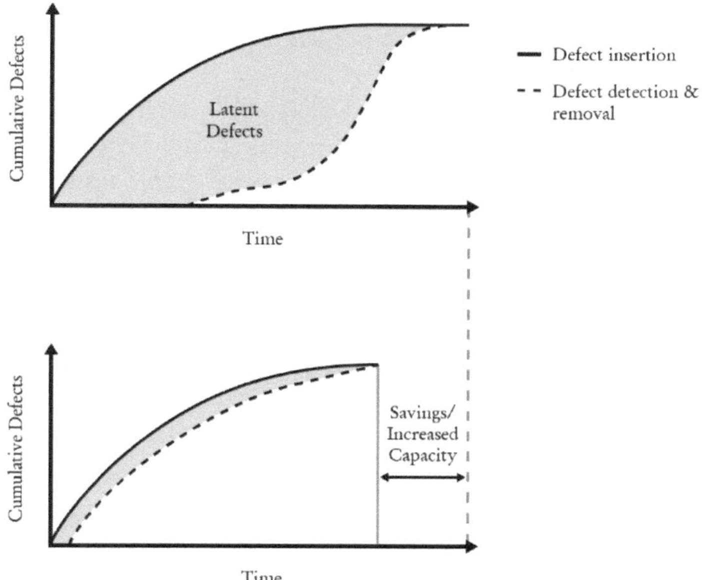

Figure 9-2
Well-run projects attempt to minimize the gap between defect insertion and defect detection and removal.

Projects that have defect-correction effort closely follow defect-creation effort run more efficiently, and as the figure shows, end up delivering in less time with less effort. No project is going to detect 100% of defects immediately, but minimizing the number of latent defects present is a useful goal even the goal can never be achieved completely.

Key Principle: Create and Use a Definition of Done

A clear Definition of Done (DoD) supports minimizing the gap between defect insertion and defection detection by ensuring that QA work on an item is performed close to all other work.

A good Definition of Done will typically include that the functionality has been coded, meets design and coding standards, has been reviewed, passes its tests, tests have been automated, and the work has been documented and integrated.

- ☐ Code Reviewed
- ☐ Static code analysis passes
- ☐ Unit tests run without error
- ☐ 70% statement coverage through unit tests
- ☐ System and integration testing complete
- ☐ Automated non-functional tests complete without error
- ☐ Builds without errors or warnings
- ☐ Any public APIs documented

Figure 9-3
An example of a Definition of Done, which determines when a backlog item is actually complete.

Teams need to define their own Definition of Done with factors that are relevant to their circumstances. In addition to the factors shown in Figure 9-3, a Definition of Done could include:

- Product Owner accepts the item
- Conforms to UI style guide
- Passes acceptance tests
- Passes performance tests
- Passes selected regression tests
- Code checked in

Multiple Definitions of Done

There are two general ways in which teams will need more than one Definition of Done.

Multiple types of DoD

It is useful or necessary to have different DoDs for different kinds of work. For example, a DoD for defects might include full regression testing, whereas a DoD for user documentation would not. Each DoD needs to implement the idea that it defines the exit criteria to the next phase and embody the principle that no more rework will be needed on an item that has met the Definition of Done.

Multiple levels of DoD

The second circumstance that calls for multiple DoDs is when it is not possible to fully complete work at one phase. In a combined hardware/software environment, for example, the first-level Definition of Done might include passing all tests in a simulation environment but not necessarily passing on the target hardware if it is not yet available. The second-level DoD would include passing all tests on the actual target hardware.

Similarly, if your software depends on another team's or a contractor's software, you might have a first-level DoD that states that all your tests pass with mock objects if the other team hasn't yet delivered the components you depend on. The second-level DoD would then state that your tests pass with the delivered components.

Although practical reasons exist to allow multiple-level DoDs, doing so creates a risk that "Done" doesn't truly mean "Done" and that poor quality and additional work will accumulate in the cracks between the different definitions. It's best to avoid this if possible.

Evolving Definition of Done

A common issue in legacy environments is that large legacy code bases cannot instantly be transformed to meet a rigorous Definition of Done. Thus, the DoD in a legacy environment might need to initially set a lower bar than it would in a greenfield environment. As the quality level of legacy code improves, the DoD can be evolved to set an increasingly high bar.

Common Issues with Definition of Done

As your teams define and implement Definitions of Done, be aware of these common issues:

DoD defines a standard that is too far from releasable. Details can vary, but the spirit of the DoD should be that when an item is declared "done" it can be released without any further work.

DoD is too large. A DoD checklist that's 50 entries long will be too unwieldy to be followed by your teams, and it won't be followed.

DoD is too ambitious for legacy systems. Avoid creating a DoD that is not possible to follow on legacy systems or that implies an amount of work greater than what has been authorized for the project.

Multi-level DoDs are too relaxed. Beware of using multi-level DoDs at all. If you do use them, be sure that the criteria for each level accurately capture "done" for that level.

Key Principle: Maintain a Potentially Releasable Level of Quality

Related to the Definition of Done, which applies to individual items, ensuring that the overall code base is kept at a potentially releasable level of quality at all times provides a quality safety net that supports efficiency in many other practices, including coding, debugging, and obtaining meaningful user feedback.

Maintaining a potentially releasable level of quality also supports the key principle that opened this chapter: minimize the gap between defect insertion and detection. If you bring the software to a releasable level of quality every 1–2 weeks, you will never allow that gap to open very wide.

Measure Rework Ratios

"Rework" refers to work on items that had previously been declared to be "done." It includes bug fixes, late changes in requirements, modifications of test cases, and other corrections to work that should have been done correctly in the first place.

Rework is disruptive to projects because the amount of rework is unpredictable, projects don't allow time for it in their plans, and it creates no additional value.

Rework is a useful proxy for inefficiency or waste on software projects. On Sequential projects, rework tends to accumulate at the end of the project, unplanned, and is therefore quite visible. On Agile projects, rework tends to accumulate and be worked off more incrementally, and it is therefore less noticeable. But it's still there, and it's useful to monitor the rework ratio.

The use of story points provides a good foundation for measuring rework. Stories can be classified as new work or rework and assigned story points. A rework ratio (R%) can be calculated from that.

Alternatively, you can set a policy that rework is not assigned story points. If the team spends much time on rework, you'll be able to see its velocity decrease because the time spent on rework does not add to the story-point count.

A measured rework percentage is an important input to the process improvement efforts described in Chapter 21, "More Effective Agile Process Improvement."

Other Considerations

Mob Programming, Swarming, and Related Practices

Some teams have experimented with mob programming, in which the whole team works on the same thing at the same time on the same computer. Others have experimented with swarming, in which the whole team works on the same story at the same time, but each team member works on their own part of the story at their own computer.

A few teams have experienced success with these practices, but overall I regard both mob programming and swarming as largely unproved niche practices that should be used selectively or not at all.

Suggested Leadership Actions

Inspect

- Review the lists of open bugs for your projects. How many open bugs are there? Does the number imply that your projects are building up a backlog of latent defects as they go, without fixing them?
- Ask your teams to show you their Definition of Done. Do they have a clear, documented definition, and are they using it? Do the details of the definition cumulatively amount to "potentially releasable"?
- Investigate whether your teams measure the percentage of rework on their projects and use it as an input for process improvement work.
- What impediments exist between what your teams are doing today and getting to "potentially releasable"? How can you help your teams address those impediments?

Adapt

- Make a plan to reduce open bug counts on your projects and then to keep the counts low.
- Work with your teams to measure the percentage of effort that's going into rework on your projects. Monitor this percentage as part of your process improvement efforts.
- Remove the impediments between what your team is doing today and getting to "potentially releasable."

Additional Resources

McConnell, Steve. 2019. Understanding Software Projects Lecture Series. *Construx OnDemand.* [Online] 2019. https://ondemand.construx.com. This series contains an extensive discussion of quality-related issues.

CHAPTER TEN

More Effective Agile Requirements Creation

For the first 25 years I worked in software development, every study I saw that examined causes of project challenge and failure found that the leading cause of problems was poor requirements—requirements that were incomplete, incorrect, contradictory, and so on. For the past 10 years, the most common cause of challenges my company has found on Agile projects has been difficulty in filling the Product Owner role, which is really about—you guessed it—requirements.

Because requirements have been such a widespread and persistent source of software project challenges, I'm going to use the next two chapters to dive deeper into requirements specifics than I have into other topics.

CHAPTER TEN

Agile Requirements Lifecycle

Compared to 25 years ago, today we have some very effective requirements practices that can be used on Agile projects. These practices help with each of the main requirements development activities:

- *Elicitation*—initial discovery of requirements.
- *Analysis*—development of a richer and more refined understanding of requirements, including priorities among them.
- *Specification*—memorialization of the requirements in a persistent form.
- *Validation*—assurance that requirements are the correct requirements (will satisfy customer needs) and that they are captured correctly.

For most of the techniques, there isn't much difference in how a team would use them for an Agile or a Sequential project. What is different is *when* the team performs the activities.

This chapter describes the elicitation and specification activities and begins the discussion of analysis. The next chapter focuses on the prioritization aspect of analysis. The main techniques for validation of requirements on Agile projects include ongoing conversations about the requirements and the end of sprint review (i.e., the working software).

What's Different About Agile Requirements?

As Karl Wiegers and Joy Beatty describe in *Software Requirements, 3rd Ed*, requirements work occurs at different times on Agile projects than it does on Sequential projects (Wiegers, 2013).

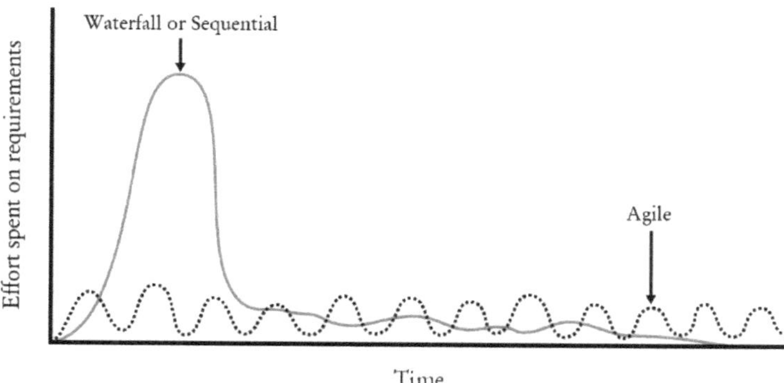

Figure 10-1

Differences in front-loading of requirements work for Agile vs. Sequential projects. Adapted from (Wiegers, 2013).

On Sequential projects, a significant percentage of requirements work is performed in a large batch at the beginning of the project. Up-front work on Agile projects is much smaller and is focused mostly on understanding the scope of requirements. Detailed refinement of individual requirements (elaboration) is deferred until shortly before development work on those requirements begins.

Figure 10-2 shows pictorially how Agile projects aim to define just the essence of each requirement at the beginning of the project, leaving most of the detailed elaboration work to be done just in time.

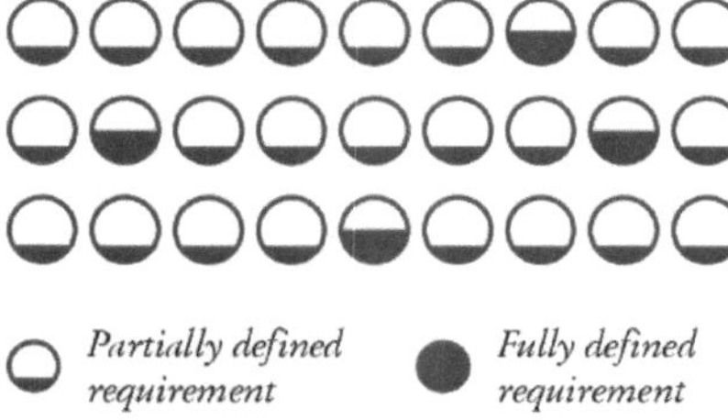

Figure 10-2

Up-front work vs. just-in-time requirements work on an Agile project. The goal on Agile projects is to avoid doing detailed requirements work up front while still covering the full breadth of requirements.

Figure 10-3 shows that on Sequential projects the details of each requirement are elaborated up front, with little requirements work left until later in the project. The whole requirement is developed early, not just the essence.

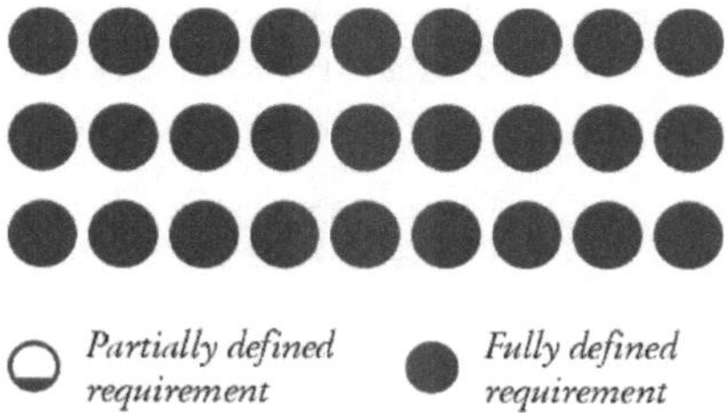

Figure 10-3

On Sequential projects, the goal is to define requirements in full detail, up front.

Detailed requirements work is performed in both Agile and Sequential approaches, but it is performed at different times. By performing the bulk of the work up front, the Sequential project is essentially saying, "I'm betting that having detailed requirements up front will add value to the rest of the project. I'm betting that working on detailed requirements up front will reduce uncertainty and that the spoilage rate of this up-front work will be acceptable." ("Spoilage" is requirements work that becomes out of date before implementation work begins.)

The Agile project is essentially saying, "I'm betting that doing end-to-end implementation work (not just requirements work) and gaining feedback will reduce uncertainty. I'm betting that doing a lot of detailed requirements work up front will create a lot of details that spoil by the time we get to implementation. The waste arising from requirements spoilage will be higher than whatever value-add there might have been from fully defining the requirements up front."

There's some truth in both arguments, and which approach works better ends up being more an economic decision than a technical one.

The challenges with defining requirements in detail up front include these:

- Requirements change, and they have to be re-elaborated between the time they're initially elaborated and the time that implementation work begins. The initial elaboration work was waste.
- Requirements are eliminated after significant elaboration work has already been done. The elaboration work was waste.
- Some requirements are overlooked, which causes problems for design and implementation approaches that are based on the assumption that requirements were defined completely or nearly completely up front. The misguided design and implementation work was waste.

Figure 10-4 shows the relationship between the requirements as originally defined and the requirements that make up the released system.

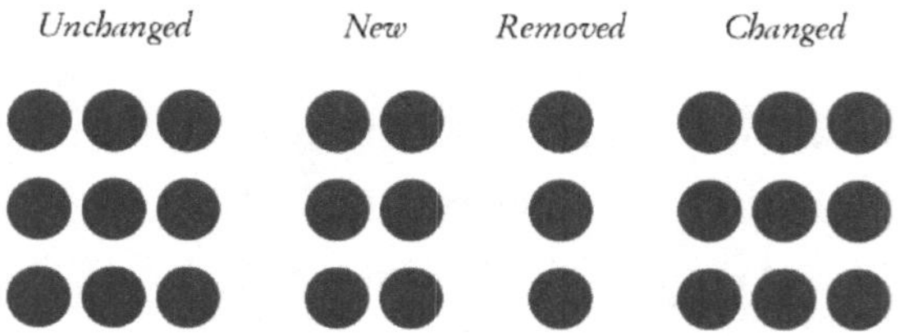

Figure 10-4

Kinds of changes in requirements over the course of a release.

In this figure, depending on when the requirements work was done, there can either be a little waste or a lot of waste.

If requirements were developed up front using a Sequential approach, new requirements are not waste but the requirements that changed or eliminated do amount to waste. The extent of the waste is shown in Figure 10-5.

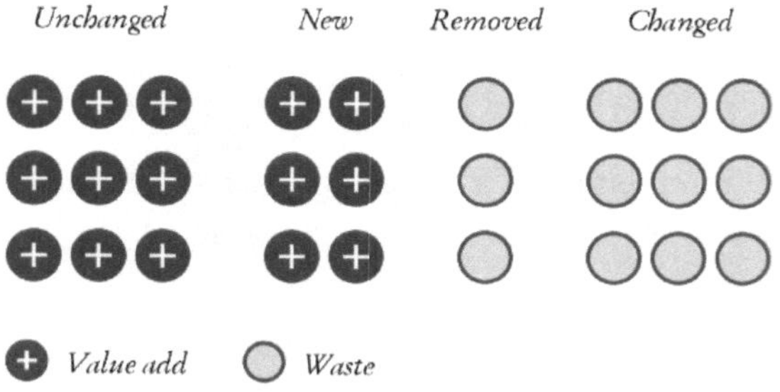

Figure 10-5

Value-add vs. waste with up-front requirements work.

As the figure shows, some of the up-front work is value-add, but the proportion of waste cannot be overlooked, especially if there is a better option. Figure 10-6 shows the contrast in value-add vs. waste for an Agile project, which addresses most of the elaboration work on a just-in-time basis.

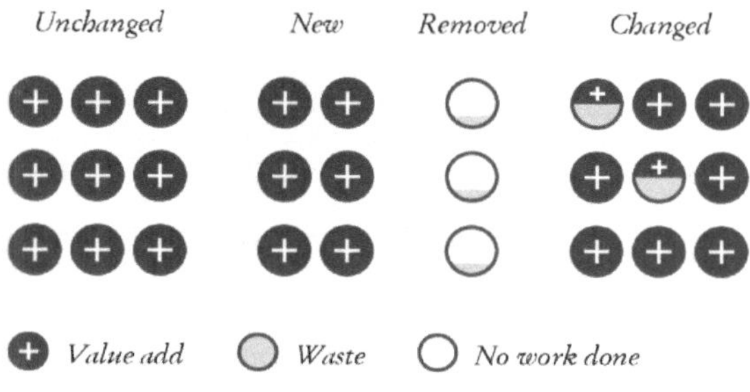

Figure 10-6

Value-add vs. waste with just-in-time requirements work.

False starts and dead ends still occur with Agile requirements, but less up-front investment in those false starts and dead ends means less waste overall.

In extreme cases, the difference in waste can be more dramatic. With a major change in project direction, for example, the Sequential project's waste looks like Figure 10-7.

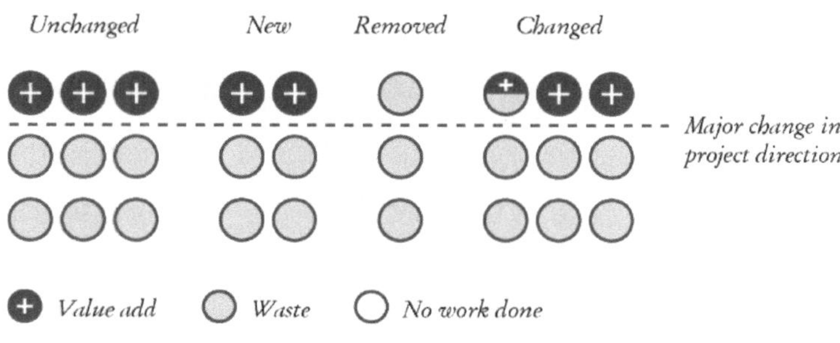

Figure 10-7

Waste with a major change in project direction on a Sequential project.

In this case, nearly all the up-front requirements work on the Sequential project is waste, whereas the Agile project invested little work in requirements that were cancelled. Figure 10-8 shows that.

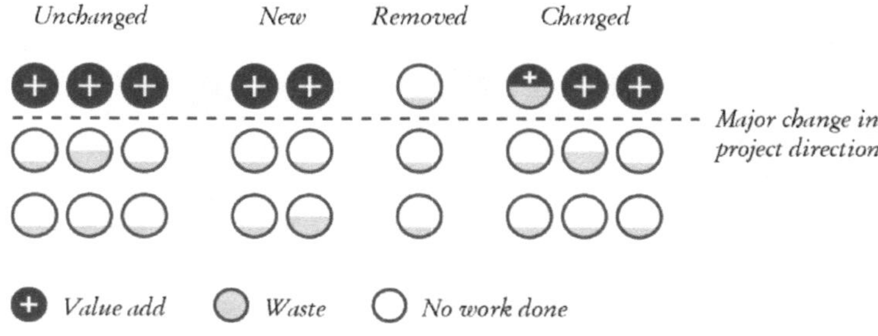

Figure 10-8
Waste with a major change in project direction on an Agile project.

In summary, requirements are not elaborated less on Agile projects, but they are elaborated later. Some Agile projects make the mistake of not actually doing the elaboration, but that is more characteristic of code-and-fix development than Agile. More effective Agile projects elaborate their requirements by using the kinds of practices described in the rest of this chapter.

Agile Requirements: Stories

Agile requirements are most commonly expressed in the form of stories, which take the form of:

As a <type of user>, I want <goal/ desire> so that <benefit>

A story is a limited, defined set of functionality. Some examples are shown in Table 10-1.

Agile projects usually rely on stories as the primary means of expressing requirements. Stories can be captured in Agile tools, in a document or spreadsheet, on index cards, or on sticky notes on a wall. Stories are refined through conversations, and the conversations should include business, development, and testing perspectives—plus other perspectives if appropriate to the story. I'll tighten up the concept of "story" after the next section.

Table 10-1 Examples of User Stories

	Type of User		Goal/ Desire		Benefit
As a	software leader	**I want to**	know my project status quantitatively	**so that**	I can keep the rest of my organization informed
As a	software leader	**I want to**	see all the current requirements in one place	**so that**	I can understand the scope of the project
As a	software leader	**I want to**	measure the productivity of my team	**so that**	I can see whether changes are helping or hurting productivity

The Agile Requirements Container: The Product Backlog

Agile requirements are typically contained in a product backlog, which contains stories, epics, themes, initiatives, features, functions, requirements, enhancements, and fixes—all the work needed to define the remainder of a project's scope. The "backlog" term is standard in Scrum. Kanban teams might call it an "input queue," but the concepts are similar.

Most teams find that having about two sprints' worth of refined backlog items beyond the current sprint provides enough detail to support workflow planning and technical implementation. For teams doing work that's mostly in

Cynefin's Complex domain, a shorter planning horizon can be more practical.

Figure 10-9 illustrates the way that the product backlog items become more refined as implementation of those backlog items approaches.

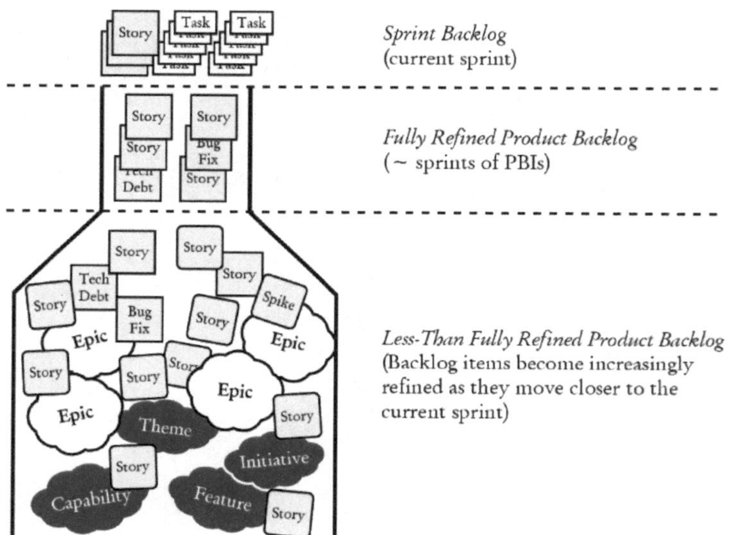

Figure 10-9

The Agile product backlog emphasizes just-in-time refinement.

What Goes into the Product Backlog?

Agile requirements terminology can be pretty loose, but the most common definitions look like this:

Requirement—an umbrella term that includes features, epics, stories, fixes, enhancements, and so on.

Feature—an increment of functionality that delivers capability or value to a business. The connotation of feature is that it requires more than one sprint to deliver. It is often described as a collection of user stories.

Epic—a story that requires more than one sprint to deliver. There is not widespread agreement on the difference between epic and feature, except that both are too large to complete in a single sprint.

Theme, capability, initiative, enhancement, etc.—because there is an expectation that the backlog will be refined, relatively amorphous items can be added to it, especially at the far end of the backlog, with the expectation that those items will be refined in due course.

User story or *story*—a description of a feature or capability described from the perspective of the person using the system. Some people make a distinction between story and user story, but usage of the two terms is not standardized—in most usages, the two terms are synonyms. Stories are commonly defined as fitting within a single sprint. If a story is discovered to require more than one sprint (which is common, through the refinement process), it is called an epic rather than a story.

Fixes, technical debt reduction, spikes—development team–oriented work that doesn't implement user requirements. This kind of work is generally called "enablers."

The terminology associated with contents of the product backlog is extensive and sometimes ambiguous. For this reason, some Agile practitioners simply refer to all backlog items as "product backlog items," or PBIs, which is a handy way of sidestepping a raft of terminology issues.

How Requirements Get into the Product Backlog

The backlog plays a key role on Agile projects, and many Agile texts are completely silent about how the Product

Owner and the rest of the Agile team is supposed to populate it.

Requirements can get into the product backlog through a variety of techniques. The overall approaches can be described as top-down or bottom-up.

Top-Down Requirements Elicitation

In the top-down approach, the requirements process begins by identifying actors, features, epics, initiatives—top-level business goals, functions and capabilities. These are then decomposed into stories. Good techniques for starting the top-down approach include:

- Create a story map
- Define a product vision
- Craft an elevator pitch
- Design the product box
- Create a lean canvas
- Design an impact map
- Identify personas

Each of these approaches is intended to define a general direction for the release, and each is intended to help generate the more detailed stories that will guide implementation.

Bottom-Up Requirements Elicitation

In the bottom-up approach, the requirements process begins by enumerating stories. These can be aggregated into themes, features, and epics. Good techniques for the bottom-up approach include:

- Hold a user story–writing workshop (which can use many of the top-down techniques)

- Conduct focus groups with typical users
- Hold requirements elicitation interviews
- Observe users performing their jobs
- Review problem reports from the current system
- Review existing requirements (if replicating functionality of an existing system)
- Review existing enhancement requests

Bottom-up approaches tend to be most useful for work on legacy systems.

Top-Down vs. Bottom-Up

When using the top-down approach, challenges arise from not diving deep enough into the details to expose the full scope of work, leaving too many details to be discovered during later backlog refinement.

With bottom-up requirements elicitation, the challenge is obtaining a meaningful view of the overall system—that is, "not being able to see the forest for the trees." You might overlook top-level constraints that override detailed work. Additional work is sometimes needed to ensure that the team's work adds up to a coherent overall direction.

The bottom-up and top-down approaches end up meeting in the middle to some degree. A workshop for writing user stories can draw in many of the top-down techniques, a product box draft can be used as a prompt in a requirements elicitation interview, and so on.

Details of specific Agile requirements elicitation practices are beyond the scope of this book. The end of this chapter contains suggestions for where to find more information.

Key Principle: Refine the Product Backlog

After the product backlog is initially populated, it needs to be "refined" on an ongoing basis so that each PBI contains enough detail to support effective sprint planning and development work. We typically want to see about two sprints' worth of fully refined PBIs in the backlog at all times, not including the work in the current sprint.

Insufficient backlog refinement can cause a number of problems for the Agile team:

- The backlog items are not defined in sufficient detail to guide the work, so the team goes in the wrong direction.
- The team spends too much time refining during the sprint and encounters too many surprises as it goes.
- The backlog items have not been updated, so the team implements out-of-date concepts of the work.
- The backlog is not prioritized properly, so the team works on lower value items and delays work on more valuable items.
- Backlog items are misestimated and are too large, so the team cannot complete its sprint commitment because items were larger than expected.
- The team might be outright starved for work because there aren't enough refined items in the backlog.

Backlog Refinement Sessions

Backlog refinement is done in a meeting or session that includes the Product Owner, Scrum Master, and the Development Team. The whole team attends so that shared understanding can be developed of the upcoming work.

Work includes discussing stories and epics, splitting epics into stories, splitting stories into smaller stories (and splitting epics into smaller epics), clarifying details of stories, defining acceptance criteria for stories, and estimating stories.

Backlog refinement meetings are typically held mid-sprint. If questions need to be clarified, that work can be done prior to the next sprint planning meeting so that open questions don't undermine sprint planning.

The Product Owner is responsible for bringing a prioritized (ordered) list of PBIs to the backlog refinement session and should have already completed most of the requirements-related elaboration work.

Definition of Ready

Just as Definition of Done helps teams avoid moving work to the next stage before it is really done, a clear, documented Definition of Ready (DoR) helps a team avoid moving requirements into development before they are really done. (You could think of Definition of Ready as a special kind of Definition of Done.)

A PBI is considered to be ready when it is:

- Understood by the Development Team well enough to decide whether it's doable in the sprint
- Estimated, and it fits into a single sprint
- Free from dependencies that would block it from being implemented during the sprint
- Defined with acceptance criteria (testable)

Teams can create their own DoR, which will be a variation on these points. The goal is to have the targeted PBIs fully refined before the next sprint planning meeting so that that meeting has all the information needed to plan effectively rather than being sidetracked by open issues.

Agile Acceptance Criteria

The Agile Manifesto said, "We prefer working software over comprehensive documentation." One of the most interesting and useful manifestations of that value has been in defining requirements acceptance criteria.

Good acceptance criteria are clear and concise, written in language the end-user understands, and verifiable. Agile has not changed any of that that. But for decades conventional wisdom has add the idea that, "Good requirements are testable." Effective Agile development extends that idea by defining acceptance criteria as a set of test cases.

One effective approach for this is Behavior Driven Development (BDD). In BDD, acceptance criteria (tests) are written in the form of:

Given <some initial context>,
When <an event occurs>,
Then <there are some outcomes>.

For example, for a requirement of "Return a list of available tables in a restaurant for a reservation request," the acceptance criteria might look like this:

Given a date, time, and size of party,
When a reservation request is made,
Then provide a list of available tables.

This style of acceptance criteria is readable by all stakeholders, including business stakeholders and technical staff. Its human readability allows the team to receive feedback about what they're building.

Specialized support tooling is then used to read descriptions and transform them into automated tests.

This sort of executable specification allows for testing correctness of the system throughout the project. Because the tests are automated, it allows tests to be conducted more frequently, which supports more frequent releases. It detects defects earlier, which provides more time to fix the defects and reduces the risk of inserting secondary regression defects during hasty, late-in-the-release-cycle defect corrections. And it avoids the inefficiency and risk of keeping acceptance criteria redundantly both in human-readable Word documents and in machine-readable traditional test cases.

Other Considerations

Requirements Fundamentals

Requirements have been a thorny issue in software development for decades. Agile has contributed useful practices to the requirements canon, but it has not changed the importance of high-quality requirements.

In Sequential development, requirements issues were conspicuous because the aggregate inefficiency was experienced all at once, cumulatively, at the end of the project. On a year-long project, if poor requirements contributed 10% inefficiency to a project, the project would be more than a month late. That pain is difficult to ignore.

In Agile development, the pain of poorly defined requirements is metabolized in smaller increments, more frequently, over the course of a project. A Scrum team that's experiencing 10% inefficiency from poorly defined requirements might simply re-do a story every few sprints. That doesn't seem as painful because the pain is not borne all at once, but the cumulative inefficiency can be just as great.

When performing reviews and retrospectives, Agile teams should be especially attentive to requirements issues. A team that finds that it's misunderstanding user stories should consider a focused effort to improve its requirements skills.

Table 10-1 Useful Requirements Practices

Acceptance Test Driven Development (ATDD)	Laddering questions
Behavior Driven Development	Lean canvas
Checklists	Personas
Context diagram	Planguage
Elevator pitch	Product box
Event lists	Product vision
Extreme characters	Prototypes
Five whys	Scenarios
Impact mapping	Story mapping
Interviews	User stories

Suggested Leadership Actions

Inspect

- Review your teams' approaches to requirements through the lens of up front vs. just in time. What would you estimate is your "requirements spoilage rate" (percentage of requirements that are out of date or need to be redefined between the time you define them and the time you implement them)?
- Are your teams using top-down or bottom-up approaches to elicit requirements? To what degree are you seeing the typical challenges described in this chapter for each of these approaches? Do the teams have plans in place to account for them?
- Attend a backlog refinement session with the goal of understanding the status of the team's backlog. Do they have enough requirements defined to support efficient sprint planning and efficient development work during their sprints?
- Investigate whether your teams have a documented Definition of Ready and are using it.
- Review the past sprint reviews and retrospectives and identify backlog items that could not be completed because of insufficient backlog refinement. Has the team taken actions to prevent that from happening in the future?

Adapt

- Take steps to create a Definition of Ready.
- Take steps to ensure product backlog refinement is occurring in a timely way.

Additional Resources

Wiegers, Karl and Joy Beatty. 2013. *Software Requirements, 3rd Ed.* Redmond, Washington : Microsoft Press, 2013.

Robertson, Robertson Suzanne and James. 2013. *Mastering the Requirements Process: Getting Requirements Right, 3rd Ed.* Upper Saddle River, New Jersey : Addison-Wesley, 2013.

Cohn, Mike. 2004. *User Stories Applied: For Agile Software Development.* s.l. : Addison-Wesley, 2004.

Adzic, Gojko and David Evans. 2014. *Fifty Quick Ideas to Improve Your User Stories.* s.l. : Neuri Consulting LLP, 2014.

Leffingwell, Dean. 2011. *Agile Software Requirements: Lean Requirements Practices for Teams, Programs, and the Enterprise.* Boston, Massachusetts : Pearson Education, Inc., 2011.

Wynne, Matt, et al. 2017. *The Cucumber Book: Behaviour-Driven Development for Testers and Developers, 2nd Ed.* s.l. : Pragmatic Programmers, 2017.

CHAPTER ELEVEN

More Effective Agile Requirements Prioritization

One of the key emphases of Agile development is to deliver incremental business functionality from highest priority to lowest. Prioritizing requirements has always been useful, but for Agile projects requirements prioritization becomes a more prominent focus. A few really effective techniques have been developed to support this.

On Agile projects, prioritization is used to decide which stories to implement and which stories not to. It's also used to order work in the product backlog, with the highest-priority stories moving toward the top of the backlog for additional refinement and implementation in the near-term sprints.

T-Shirt Sizing

As I discussed in my book *Software Estimation: Demystifying the Black Art* (McConnell, 2006), T-shirt sizing is a useful way to prioritize partially refined functionality based on approximate ROI.

In this approach, technical staff classifies each story's size (development cost) relative to other stories as Small, Medium, Large, or Extra Large. ("Stories" can also be features, requirements, epics, and so on.) In parallel, the customer, marketing, sales, or other nontechnical stakeholders classify the stories' business value on the same scale. These two sets of entries are then combined as shown in Table 11-1.

Table 11-1 Using T-Shirt Sizing to Classify Stories by Business Value and Development Cost

Story	Business Value	Development Cost
Story A	Large	Small
Story B	Small	Large
Story C	Large	Large
Story D	Medium	Medium
Story E	Medium	Large
Story F	Large	Medium
...		
Story ZZ	Small	Small

Creating this sort of relationship between business value and development cost allows the nontechnical stakeholder to say things like, "If the development cost of Story B is Large, I don't want it because the value is only Small." This is a tremendously useful decision to be able to make early in the elaboration of that story. If you were instead to carry that story through some amount of refinement, architecture, design, and so on, you would be expending effort on a story that ultimately isn't cost-justifiable. The value of a quick "No" in software is high. T-Shirt sizing allows for early-in-the-project decisions to rule out stories, without needing to carry those stories through further elaboration.

The discussion about what to carry forward and what to cut is easier if stories can be sorted into a rough cost/benefit order. Typically, this is done by assigning a "net business value" number based on the combination of development cost and business value. Table 11-2 shows one possible scheme for assigning a net business value to each combination. You can use this scheme or come up with one that more accurately reflects the value arising from combinations of development cost and business value in your environment.

Table 11-2 Approximate Net Business Value Based on Ratio of Development Cost to Business Value

	Development Cost			
Business Value	*Extra Large*	*Large*	*Medium*	*Small*
Extra Large	0	4	6	7
Large	-4	0	2	3
Medium	-6	-2	0	1
Small	-7	-3	-1	0

This sort of net benefit lookup table allows you to add a third column to the original cost/benefit table and to sort that table by net business value, as shown in Table 11-3.

Table 11-3 Sorting T-Shirt Sizing Estimates by Approximate Net Business Value

Story	**Business Value**	**Develop-ment Cost**	**Approximate Net Busi-ness Value**
Story A	L	S	3
Story F	L	M	2
Story C	L	L	0
Story D	M	M	0
Story ZZ	S	S	0
Story E	M	L	-2
…			
Story B	S	L	-3

The "Approximate Net Business Value" column is what it says—an *approximation.* I don't suggest just counting down the list and drawing a line. The value of sorting by approximate business value is that it supports getting quick "definitely yes" responses for the stories at the top of the list and quick "definitely no" decisions for the stories at the bottom. You'll still need to discuss the items in the middle. Because the net business values are approximate, you'll occasionally see cases in which a story that has a value of 1 is a better idea than a story that has a value of 2 when you look at the details.

T-Shirt Sizing and Story Points

This discussion of T-shirt sizing has used the same T-shirt scale for development cost and business value. If stories have been refined enough to assign story points, the technique works equally well if story points are used for the "T-shirt sizes" of the development costs and the business values are still expressed in true T-shirt sizes. The purpose of T-shirt sizing is to calculate the approximate net business value so that the list can be sorted, with the highest-ROI ideas rising to the top. This can be done regardless of what scale is used for development cost.

Story Mapping

Product backlogs often consist of dozens or hundreds of stories. It's easy for priorities to get confused in large backlogs, and it's easy for the collection of items delivered at the end of each sprint to be pretty incoherent even if, individually, they represent the highest-priority backlog items.

Story mapping is a powerful technique for prioritizing the sequence in which stories are delivered while simultaneously shaping the collections of stories into coherent packages (Patton, 2014). It also helps with elicitation, analysis, and specification of requirements, and it becomes an aid to status tracking during development.

Story mapping is conducted with the whole team and consists of three steps:

1. Capture major chunks of functionality on sticky notes, and arrange them in a prioritized line from left to right, highest priority to lowest. Major chunks of functionality will consist of features, epics/big stories, themes, initia-

tives, and other large-grain requirements. I'll refer to these generically as epics in the rest of this discussion.

2. Decompose top-level epics into steps or themes. This elaboration of the epics does not change the prioritization of the epics.
3. Decompose each of the steps or themes into stories captured on sticky notes. Arrange these below each step or theme in priority order.

This process results in a story map that lists requirements in priority order both from left to right and top to bottom.

The following sections describe these steps in more detail.

Step 1: Prioritize Epics and Other Top-Level Functionality

Top-level functionality is prioritized using sticky notes from left to right, as shown in Figure 11-1.

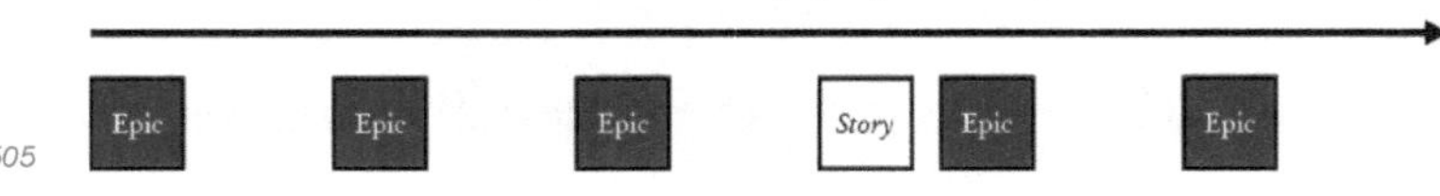

Figure 11-1

Story mapping begins with listing epics (and other top-level features) in priority order from left to right.

The epics can be prioritized using T-shirt sizing or other techniques, possibly including Weighted Shortest Job First (WSJF), discussed in Chapter 20, "More Effective Agile Portfolio Management."

After being ordered from left to right, lower-priority epics on the right side of the story map might not be important enough to be included in the release at all. If they are important enough to be included in the release, they still might not be important enough to be included in a minimum viable product (MVP).

Step 2: Decompose Top-Level Epics into Steps or Themes

Most epics will be intuitively describable as sequential steps. Some will not consist of sequential steps and can be decomposed into themes.

Top-Level Priority (High to Low)

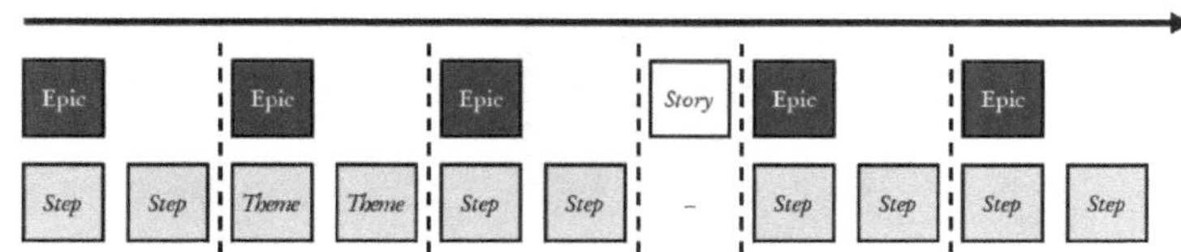

Figure 11-2

Story mapping enumerates steps or themes below epics, which doesn't change the prioritization order of the epics.

This second-level decomposition into steps and themes is called "the backbone" in story mapping. Walking through a description of the backbone should provide a coherent description of overall functionality.

Step 3: Decompose Each Step or Theme into Prioritized Stories

Below the backbone, each step or theme is further decomposed into one or more stories. These are arranged in priority order from top to bottom. These more detailed priorities can be established using T-shirt sizing or more informal judgment by the team.

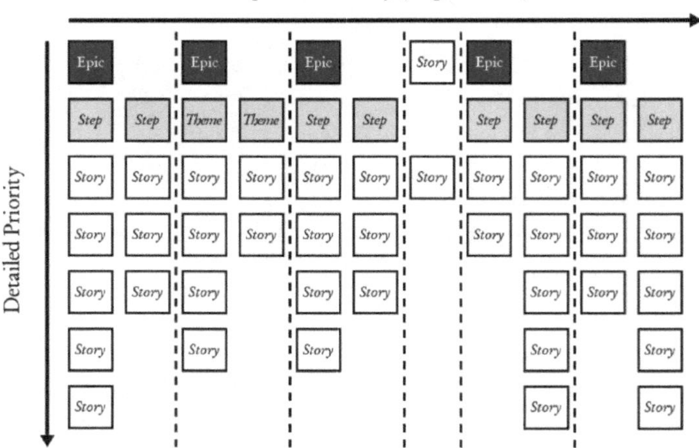

Figure 11-3

The team decomposes each step or theme into stories and sorts them in priority order.

The vertical stacks of stories under each step or theme are called “ribs” in story mapping.

The collection of the shallow set of stories immediately below the backbone makes up a minimal implementation of end-to-end functionality and is called the “walking skeleton.”

The walking skeleton is intended to be a coherent subset of functionality, but it is just a skeleton and is not normally sufficient to be a minimum viable product (MVP). The MVP is typically defined as including a subset of stories below the walking skeleton.

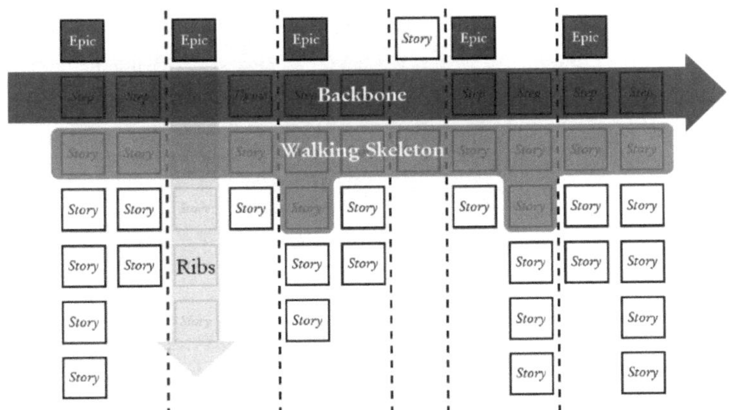

Figure 11-4
The horizontal slice of functionality immediately below the backbone makes up the minimal implementation of the release, called the "walking skeleton."

Story Mapping and User Roles

I've shown an example of Story Mapping in which epics are decomposed into steps. A useful variation can be to start with user roles at the top, prioritize those from left to right, and then decompose epics below those.

Benefits of Story Mapping

Story mapping provides powerful support for the Agile approach to requirements in which requirements are refined only shortly before they are implemented.

The act of walking through the stories from left to right and top to bottom often exposes missing steps in an epic, misunderstandings of priorities, and other mistakes.

One of the more common failure modes my company has observed with Agile projects is delivering functionality in priority order but missing the big-picture view—delivering long lists of fine-grain functionality that don't add up to a coherent release. By defining a backbone, walking skeleton, and MVP, the Development Team obtains clear direction for delivering prioritized functional *and* coherent functionality.

Story Mapping as an Example of an Information Radiator

Effective Agile practices emphasize making work *visible*—not just accessible on a web page but actually a visible part of the work environment. A story map on the wall is a constant reminder of team priorities, current assignments, and future work flow. Agile teams refer to this kind of display as an "information radiator." Forsgren, Humble, and Kim's research has found that the use of visual displays of this kind are necessary parts of achieving improved delivery performance (Forsgren, 2018).

Story Mapping as an Example of the Agile Pendulum Swing

Story mapping is a fascinating example of how the software development pendulum has swung from pure Sequential development to early Agile, and it has now swung back to a *better Agile*. Early Agile development avoided doing up-front requirements work at all costs, leaving requirements to be done just in time—and only just in time. Story mapping, strongly associated with Agile development, is an approach for organizing and prioritizing requirements *up front*. But it is not an old, Sequential, fully elaborated requirements-up-front practice. It is a practice that helps define the broad scope of a release up front and then continues to provide prioritization and guidance for incremental requirements refinement throughout the release.

Story mapping is a terrific example of the way that Sequential development and Agile development can be synthesized to provide the best of both worlds.

Other Considerations

As with requirements elicitation, requirements prioritization has been a thorny issue for decades. In addition to t-shirt sizing and story mapping, consider these useful techniques.

Dot Voting

In dot voting, each stakeholder is given a fixed number of dots—for example, 10 dots. Stakeholders then allocate their dots among requirements any way they see fit. A stakeholder can place all 10 dots on one requirement or one dot each on 10 different requirements, or 5 on one and one each on the rest—anything is possible. The technique provides a quick way to discover the priorities of a group.

MoSCoW

"MoSCoW" is a mnemonic for Must have, Should have, Could have, Won't have. It is a useful method of partitioning proposed requirements into categories.

MVE

MVE is an acronym for Minimum Viable Experiment, which refers to the smallest release that can be used to provide valuable feedback to the team. MVE is supportive of work in Cynefin's Complex domain; it amounts to a probe that's used to explore a possible product direction.

Weighted Shortest Job First (WSJF)

WSJF is a technique for maximizing value based on the sequence in which work is performed. WSJF is discussed in Chapter 20, "More Effective Agile Portfolio Management."

Suggested Leadership Actions

Inspect

- Investigate the techniques your teams are using for requirements prioritization. Do the techniques support implementing based on ROI order?
- Investigate whether your teams are implementing functionality purely on a fine-grain, descending business value basis without any consideration of the big picture.

Adapt

- Work with your teams to adopt a technique for prioritizing product backlog items—either T-shirt sizing or story mapping.
- Work with your teams to implement story mapping for the purpose of supporting coherent packages of functionality.

Additional Resources

Patton, Jeff. 2014. *User Story Mapping: Discover the Whole Story, Build the Right Product.* s.l. : O'Reilly Media, 2014.

McConnell, Steve. 2006. *Software Estimation: Demystifying the Black Art.* Redmond, Washington : Microsoft Press, 2006.

CHAPTER TWELVE

More Effective Agile Testing

Agile development has shifted the traditional test emphasis in four ways. First, it has increased the emphasis on testing by developers. Second, it has emphasized front-loading testing, with an emphasis on testing functionality immediately after it is created. It has also emphasized test automation. Finally, it has emphasized testing as a means of refining requirements.

These four emphases provide an important safety net for Agile's other emphases, such as just-in-time design and implementation. Without the safety net of a comprehensive automated test suite, the constantly changing design and code environment would give rise to a tidal wave of defects—many of them undetected and going into the latent defect pool described in Chapter 9, "More Effective Agile Quality." With the automated test safety net, most defects are detected immediately after they are created, supporting the goal of minimizing the gap between defect creation and defect detection.

The following sections describe what we have seen as the most effective test practices for Agile projects.

Key Principle: Integrate Testers into the Development Teams

The organization of testing staff has been a moving target my entire career. Once upon a time, testers were integrated into development teams and reported to the development manager. That was found to be problematic because the development managers would pressure testers to, "Stop finding so many defects." That resulted in the customers finding them instead.

For several years after that phase, testers were separated into their own group, often sat in a different area, and didn't report to the development manager any more. They reported through a different reporting structure that usually didn't converge with the reporting structure for developers until the level of Director or VP.

This structure created multiple problems. It contributed to an antagonistic relationship between development and testing, as well as to a dynamic in which developers abdicated responsibility for testing their own code.

In the next phase of the evolution of the organization of testing staff, testers continued to report separately, but they were seated with developers to support a more collaborative relationship. Developers would give testers private builds to test, testers would write test cases and share them with developers, and developers would run their code against the test cases and fix many defects before they officially checked in their code. This arrangement worked pretty well for its time in minimizing the gap between defect insertion and defect detection.

Today, two factors influence the current approach to test organization: the rise of Agile development, and the rise of automated testing.

Agile development emphasizes developers testing their own work, which has led some organizations to respond by eliminating testing as a specialization and decreeing that, "Every development staff member must test their own work." That's good as far as it goes, but it overlooks the need for testing that is more sophisticated and more cross-cutting than will typically be created by developers testing their own work. Test specialists still have a role to play in creating and maintaining those kinds of tests.

The rise in automated testing has led to an increase in the effort that's typically devoted to test (along with an increase in the value of the tests). The workload required by automation gives test specialists another useful role to play.

In recent years, we have sometimes seen the *de facto* organization of test on the ground work better than the *de jure* organization of testing on the org chart. When an organization has officially discontinued the role of tester, we still see Agile teams containing technical staff members who are more test oriented along with those who are more development oriented. We see staff members formerly classified as testers primarily focusing on integration tests, load tests, and other cross-cutting kinds of tests. We also see them shouldering a higher percentage of the test automation work than their more development-oriented team members. All things considered, this is healthy!

As discussed in Chapter 6, "More Effective Agile Teams," effective Agile development depends on creating cross-functional teams, which includes testing. Testers should work side by side with developers throughout the software development and delivery process.

Key Principle: Use Automated Tests, Created by the Development Team

The development team should be writing automated tests, which are incorporated into an automated build/deploy system. The ideal is to have multiple levels and types of testing, including unit tests, API tests, integration tests, UI layer tests, acceptance tests, simulations, support for mocking, random inputs and data, and so on.

Tests are written by the *team*, which in a cross-functional team can mean either developers or testers or former testers. The ideal is to have developers write unit tests before any changes to the code. Test development and automation are inherent aspects of backlog item implementation that are included in effort estimates.

The team should maintain an on-demand test environment that supports automated testing. A combination of automated unit testing (code-level tests) and user-level testing should be a core attribute of any Definition of Done.

A developer should be able to run unit test suites for a complete component of the product within a few minutes, either on a shared team build server or on the developer's machine.

A development team should have the capability to run a complete test pass—including all automated unit- and user-level checks—within an hour or two. The complete test pass should be run multiple times per day.

A sophisticated dev org should have the ability to support continuous integration (CI) by running all automated tests every time a check-in is made. For large projects, that requires numerous virtual environments ganging up to run test suites in parallel, which in turn requires a dedicated team that builds, maintains, and extends the CI server by incorporating test suites from disparate teams.

Large, high-profile companies like Amazon and Netflix are able to support rapid, continuous testing because they have teams that focus solely on this capability, they have invested heavily in computer hardware, and they have developed their capabilities over many years. Companies that are just getting started with CI, or that do not have the needs of an Amazon or Netflix, should scale their expectations appropriately.

Inability to develop an ideal test suite should not be taken as a reason not to create automated tests. We've seen teams that have inherited poor-quality code bases put basic smoke tests in place, slowly backfill automated tests, and realize significant gains even from a small amount of automation.

Other Keys to Effective Agile Testing

Aside from including testers on the development teams and using automating tests, keep in mind these other keys to effective Agile testing.

Measure Code Coverage

Writing test cases before writing the code ("test-first") can be a useful discipline, but we've found that, for new code bases, code-coverage measurement of unit tests combined with downstream test automation is more critical. A unit test code-coverage percentage of 70% is a useful, practical level to aim for with new code. Code coverage of 100% by unit tests is rare and usually far past the point of diminishing returns.

For organizations my company has worked with, best of breed typically approaches approximately a 1:1 ratio of test code to production code, which includes both unit test code and higher-level test code.

Beware of Abuse of Test Coverage Measures

We have found that measures like "70% statement coverage" are prone to abuse more frequently than you might expect. We've seen teams deactivate failing test cases to increase their pass ratios or create test cases that always return success.

In this case, it's more effective to fix the system than the person. This behavior suggests that the teams believe that development work is a higher priority than test work. Leadership needs to communicate that test and QA work is as important as development work. You should help your teams understand the purpose and value of the tests and emphasize that a number like 70% is simply an indicator—it is not the goal itself.

Monitor Static Code Metrics

Code coverage and other test metrics are useful, but they don't tell the entire quality story of a project. Static code quality metrics are also important: cyclomatic complexity, depth of decision nesting, number of routine parameters, file size, folder size, routine length, use of magic numbers, embedded SQL, duplicate or copied code, quality of comments, adherence to coding standards, and so on. These measures provide hints about which areas of code might need additional work to maintain quality.

Write Test Code with Care

Test code should follow the same code-quality standards as production code. It should use good naming, avoid magic numbers, be well factored, avoid duplication, have consistent formatting, and so on.

Prioritize Maintaining the Test Suites

Test suites have a tendency to degrade over time, and it isn't uncommon to find test suites in which a high percentage of the tests have been turned off. The team should include review and maintenance of the test suite as an integral cost of its ongoing development work. This is essential for supporting the goal of keeping the software close to a potentially releasable level of quality at all times—that is, for keeping defects from getting out of control.

Have the Separate Test Organization Create and Maintain Acceptance Tests

For companies that still maintain separate test organizations, it's useful to have that organization assume primary responsibility for creating and maintaining acceptance tests. The development team will still create and run acceptance tests; continuing to do that provides important support for minimizing the gap between defect insertion and defect detection. But it will have secondary responsibility for that kind of work.

Continue to Use Manual Tests as Needed

Manual tests continue to have a role in the form of exploratory testing, usability testing, and other kinds of manual tests.

Other Considerations

Pair Programming

Pair programming is a practice in which two developers sit side by side, one writing code and the other playing a role of real-time reviewer. The roles are sometimes described as pilot and navigator. Pair programming is especially associated with Extreme Programming.

Industry data on pair programming has shown for many years that the output of two people working as a pair is roughly comparable to the total output of two people working individually, the quality is higher, and the work is completed more quickly (Williams, 2002), (Boehm, 2004).

Despite it being strongly associated with Agile development, I have not emphasized pair programming as a more effective Agile practice because in my experience most developers do not prefer to do most of their work in pairs. The result is that pair programming in most organizations has settled into being a selectively used niche practice. If I had a team that wanted to use pair programming extensively, I would support that, but I wouldn't insist on it.

Suggested Leadership Actions

Inspect

- Review whether your teams' approaches to automated testing include defining standards for ideal test coverage and minimum acceptable test coverage.
- Interview your team members to understand your teams' *de facto* test organization (as opposed to what's shown on the org chart).
- Determine tests your teams are performing manually. Does your team need a plan for which of these manual tests can be automated?

Adapt

- Make a plan to ensure the test function is incorporated as an integral part of your development teams.
- Define a goal level for test automation on each of your projects. Create plans to achieve those levels over the next 3–12 months.

Additional Resources

Crispin, Lisa and Janet Gregory. 2009. *Agile Testing: A Practical Guide for Testers and Agile Teams.* s.l. : Addison-Wesley Professional, 2009.

Forsgren, Nicole, et al. 2018. *Accelerate: The Science of Lean Software and DevOps: Building and Scaling High Performing Technology Organizations.* Portland, OR : IT Revolution, 2018. This book summarizes current data on the most effective Agile testing practices.

Stuart, Jenny and Melvin Perez. 2018. Retrofitting Legacy Systems with Unit Tests. [Online] July 2018. https://www.construx.com/whitepapers.

Feathers, Michael. 2004. *Working Effectively with Legacy Code.* Upper Saddle River, New Jersey : Prentice Hall PTR, 2004.

CHAPTER THIRTEEN

More Effective Agile Delivery

Delivery is the activity in which the rest of the development process comes together. As such, delivery provides a useful lens through which to discuss several aspects of more effective Agile development.

In this chapter I refer to both *delivery* and *deployment.* "Delivery" refers to preparing the software in every way needed to make it ready for deployment but not actually deploying it. "Deployment" refers to taking that last step to put the software into production.

The last step required to get to delivery is integration. In Agile development, the goal is to have both continuous integration (CI) and continuous delivery or deployment (CD). Continuous integration is not literally "continuous." The term is used to mean that developers are checking code into a shared repository often—typically multiple times per day. Likewise, continuous delivery does not literally mean "continuous." In practice, it means delivery that is frequent and automated.

Key Principle: Automate Repetitive Activities

Software development activities tend to flow from more open-ended, creative, nondeterministic activities, such as requirements and design, to more closed-ended, deterministic activities, such as automated testing, commit to trunk, user acceptance testing, staging, and production. People are good at the more open-ended upstream activities that require thinking, and computers are good at the more deterministic downstream activities that need to be done repetitively.

The closer you get to delivery and deployment, the more sense it makes to automate the activities to be performed by computers.

For some companies the ideal is fully automated deployment, which requires a fully automated deployment pipeline, including automating repetitive tasks. Figure 13-1 shows which tasks can potentially be automated.

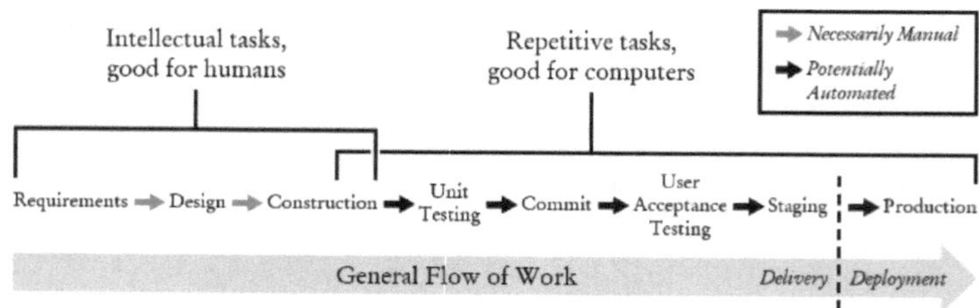

Figure 13-1

The closer software work gets to deployment, the better suited it is for automation.

The potential for frequency of deployment is essentially unlimited. For several years Amazon has been deploying every few seconds, with as many as 1,000 deployments per hour (Velocity Culture (The Unmet Challenge in Ops), June 16, 2011). Most organizations do not have any business reason to deploy anywhere near this often, but Amazon's performance shows that virtually any frequency of deployment is possible.

As Figure 13-1 suggests, the key idea in achieving automated deployment is to separate requirements, design, and construction, which can't be automated, from delivery and deployment, which can be.

Automating the later stages of the pipeline provides the benefits of increased efficiency and faster deployment. There is also a human benefit. If you consider the effect of automation through the lens of Autonomy, Mastery, and Purpose, automation also increases motivation. It eliminates a repetitive task that offers no opportunity for growth, and it frees up time that can be applied to upstream activities that do offer opportunity for growth.

Work Practices That Support CI/CD

Several work practices are required to support CI/CD, some of which have been discussed in earlier chapters.

Automate Almost Everything

To fully achieve CI/CD, the entire development environment needs to be automated. This includes versioning artifacts that might not otherwise be versioned: code, system configurations, application configurations, build, and configuration scripts.

Increase Emphasis on Automated Testing

The automated test environment should support each proposed change passing automated tests of several different types, including unit tests, API tests, integration tests, UI layer tests, tests for random inputs, tests for random data, load testing, and so on.

A major goal of CI/CD is to automatically detect and reject changes that are unacceptable due to error introduction or unacceptable performance degradation.

Increase Priority on Deployment

Maintaining the automated deployment pipeline requires effort, and for CI/CD to work, the team must prioritize keeping the system in a deployable state over doing new work (Humble, 2015).

Broaden Your Definition of Done

While DoD is an important concept on any project, the specifics become more important in a CI/CD environment.

- ☐ All the PBIs in the product increment satisfy the acceptance criteria
- ☐ Static code analysis passes
- ☐ Unit tests run without error
- ☐ 70% statement coverage through unit tests
- ☐ System and integration testing complete
- ☐ All regression tests passed
- ☐ ...
- ☐ Demonstrated in production-like environment (staging)
- ☐ Code is in the version control trunk and is releasable

Figure 13-2
Example Definition of Done for a CI/CD environment.

In a CI/CD environment, DoD needs to include standards for unit tests, acceptance tests, regression tests, staging, and revision control.

Emphasize Incremental Work Practices

Several steps need to be taken to support of the goal of minimizing the gap between defect insertion and defect detection:

- Commit code frequently (at least daily, preferably more often).
- Don't commit broken code.
- Fix breaks in the deployment pipeline immediately, including broken builds.
- Write automated developer tests with the code.
- All tests must pass.

These practices are useful in assuring that your team's software is in a releasable state every time a new feature is added or a correction is made.

Use Continuous Deployment as a Yardstick for Overall Development Effectiveness

Humans repetitively doing tasks that could be performed by computers is a form of waste. The lead time for getting changes from code change to production is a useful measurement proxy for how much manual effort is occurring throughout that pipeline.

Measuring deployment lead time can lead to increases in test automation; simplification and automation of the build, release, and deployment process; and a shift in architecture focus to designing applications with testability and deployability in mind. It can also lead to developing and deploying functionality in smaller batches.

Humble, Molesky, and O'Reilly recommend, "If it hurts, do it more often and bring the pain forward" (Humble, 2015). In other words, if it hurts, automate it so that it will stop hurting. For downstream activities that are amenable to automation, this is excellent advice.

Benefits of CI/CD

CI/CD produces both obvious and not-so-obvious benefits. The obvious benefits include getting new functionality into the hands of users faster and more often.

The not-so-obvious benefits of CI/CD might be more significant.

Teams learn faster, because they go through the develop-test-release-deploy cycle more often, which provides more frequent learning opportunities.

The penalty for errors declines, because "ease of deployment" also implies "ease of rolling back a faulty deployment." Errors are more easily reversible. This supports the organizational goal of decriminalizing errors.

Defects are detected closer to when they are introduced, so they cost less to fix, as discussed in Chapter 9, "More Effective Agile Quality."

Teams experience lower stress because push-button releases become easy, without any fear of human error causing the release to fail.

Finally, as described earlier in this chapter, CI/CD can increase motivation by allowing teams to spend more time on work that provides higher opportunity for growth.

Other Considerations

Continuous Delivery

The phrase "CI/CD" has become common in the software industry, which implies that organizations are routinely doing *both* continuous integration and continuous delivery. However, we do not see most organizations practicing the "CD" part of CI/CD. DZone Research reports that while 50% of organizations believe they have implemented CD, only 18% actually meet the textbook definition (DZone Research, 2015).

CI is a prerequisite for CD, so we have found that it makes sense to get CI right first. Despite much recent attention on environments like Netflix and Amazon, which deploy hundreds of times per day, environments that deploy weekly, monthly, quarterly, or less often are common and will be for the foreseeable future. You might be working on embedded systems, on combined hardware/software products, on FDA-regulated systems, or in an enterprise space that can't accept frequent releases. However, you can still benefit from automating the repetitive parts of CI. You might also benefit from the discipline associated with continuous delivery even if continuous deployment will never be desirable.

This is an area where the concept of the Agile boundary is useful—you might have good reasons to draw your Agile boundary so that it includes CI but doesn't include CD.

Suggested Leadership Actions

Inspect

- Familiarize yourself with the extent of automation in your delivery/deployment pipeline.
- Interview your teams to determine how much of their effort is going into repetitive delivery/deployment activities that could be automated.
- Inventory the activities in your delivery/deployment process that are still being done manually. Which activities are preventing your teams from having push-button deliveries?
- Investigate to determine whether your teams' work is planned to a level that supports frequent integration.

Adapt

- Encourage your staff to integrate their work frequently, at least daily.
- Create a Definition of Done that supports automated delivery/deployment.
- Create a plan for your teams to automate as much of their build and deployment environments as they can.
- Communicate to your staff that their work to keep the delivery/deployment pipeline working is higher priority than creating new functionality.

Additional Resources

Forsgren, Nicole, et al. 2018. *Accelerate: The Science of Lean Software and DevOps: Building and Scaling High Performing Technology Organizations.* Portland, OR : IT Revolution, 2018.

Humble, Jez, et al. 2015. *Lean Enterprise: How High Performance Organizations Innovate at Scale.* Sebastopol, CA : O'Reilly Media, 2015.

Nygard, Michael T. 2018. *Release It!: Design and Deploy Production-Ready Software, 2nd Ed.* s.l. : Pragmatic Bookshelf, 2018.

MORE EFFECTIVE AGILE ORGANIZATIONS

CHAPTER FOURTEEN

More Effective Agile Leadership

Agile enthusiasts often refer to Agile implementations as depending on "servant leadership." I believe this to be true, but I also believe it is too vague to be specifically useful for Agile adoptions. More specific guidance is required. Whether you've decided to go full-stack Agile or adopt Agile less extensively, leadership is a make-or-break aspect of Agile implementations, so this chapter is full of key principles.

Key Principle: Manage to Outcomes, Not Details

Organizations live and die based on the commitments they make and the commitments they keep. Effective Agile implementations consist of commitments both to and from the teams and both to and from leadership.

Agile teams (specifically Scrum teams) commit to leadership that they will deliver their sprint goal at the end of each sprint. In a high-fidelity Scrum implementation, the commitment is seen as absolute—the team will work mightily to live up to its sprint goals.

In return, leadership commits to the Scrum team that the sprint is sacrosanct. Leadership will not change requirements or otherwise disrupt the team while it's in the middle of a sprint. In traditional Sequential projects, this was not a reasonable expectation because the project cycles were so long and circumstances were bound to change. In Scrum projects, it's entirely reasonable because sprints are typically only 1–2 weeks long. If the organization can't maintain its focus without changing its mind during this time, the organization has larger problems than whether its Scrum implementation is going to work.

The idea of treating teams and sprints as black boxes and managing only the inputs and outputs from the sprints has the desirable side effect of forcing business leaders into less of a management posture and more of a leadership posture. Business leaders need to give direction to the teams, explain the purpose of the work, elaborate the priorities of different objectives, and then set the teams free to amaze them with the outcomes.

Key Principle: Express Clear Purpose with Commander's Intent

Autonomy and purpose are connected because a team cannot have meaningful, healthy autonomy unless it understands the purpose of its work. A self-managed team needs to make the vast majority of decisions internally. It has the cross-functional skills and the authority to do so. However, if it does not have a clear understanding of the purpose of its work, its decisions will be misguided (literally).

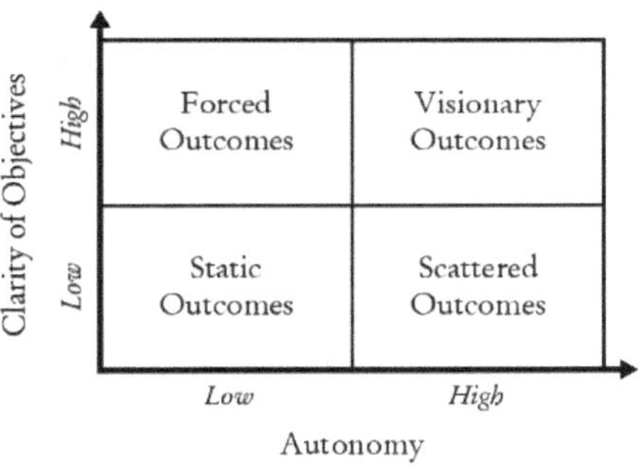

Figure 14-1
Autonomy vs. clarity of objectives.

The US military uses a notion of "Commander's Intent," which refers to a public statement of the desired end state, the purpose of the operation, and the key tasks to be accomplished. Commander's Intent is specifically useful in cases where events are not unfolding as originally planned, communication is disrupted, and a team needs to make a decision without the ability to confer higher up in the chain of command.

Your goal in a software context is similar. Communication with company leadership will probably not be forcibly disrupted, but often company leadership is not readily accessible for extended periods of time,[5] events are not unfolding as originally planned, and the team still needs to make a de-

[5] I once worked with a software executive who met with his boss only 30 minutes every six months.

cision. In those circumstances teams benefit from having a "guiding light" or "north star" or "Commander's Intent" from which they can obtain direction.

A good description of Commander's Intent will include the following:

- A statement of the reasons and motivation for the project or initiative; the purpose.
- A vivid visualization of the desired end state. It should allow team members to understand what success looks like and their part in achieving it.

An organization that wants to become Agile needs to develop the ability to describe purpose clearly. Its managers should focus on leading through objectives rather than managing by focusing on details.

> *"Don't tell people how to do things. Tell them what to do and let them surprise you with their results."*
>
> —George S. Patton

Key Principle: Prioritize, and Communicate Priorities

Effective Agile leaders support their teams by communicating unambiguous priorities. We've seen many organizations that prioritize everything as highest priority and leave it to the teams to figure it out. Or they reprioritize too frequently. Or they prioritize at too fine a level of detail. Or they refuse to prioritize at all. These mistakes are both exceedingly common and exceedingly ineffective.

Refusal to prioritize is a sign of weak leadership. It amounts to abdicating responsibility for making decisions. If you care about what gets done, you have to make decisions about priorities and then communicate those decisions to your teams unambiguously.

Frequent reprioritization can be just as damaging. Frequent changes in priorities undermine both the team's sense of autonomy and its sense of purpose. Leaders should ask themselves, "Will this reprioritization matter six months from now?" If it won't, it isn't important enough to randomize the team.

Commander's intent is a good lens through which to view the appropriate level of prioritization. The leader should define what success looks like—objectives, outcomes, impacts, and benefits—but stop short of defining details.

This is an area in which an effective Agile implementation can highlight an organization's weaknesses in ways that are threatening to its leaders. We have occasionally seen leaders shut down Agile implementations because the focus on frequent delivery (or lack thereof) highlights the leader's inability to provide clear priorities to their teams.

It's impossible to overstate how important this point is. If you are not effectively prioritizing your teams' work, you are not leading. Your projects will achieve results far short of the results they could achieve—and far short of the results that your teams deserve. The organization that wants to be effective will not avoid the discomfort that can arise from shining a bright light on prioritization weaknesses—it will instead use the discomfort as motivation to improve.

Key Principle: Focus on Throughput, Not Activity

Ineffective leaders tend to focus more on the perception of progress than the reality of progress. But not all motion is progress, and busy-ness is often a poor proxy for results.

The goal of an effective organization should be to maximize *throughput*—the rate at which work is completed—not the rate at which work is started or the level of activity. Leaders must accept that some amount of slack is necessary to maximize throughput (DeMarco, 2002).

One reason Scrum keeps accountability at the team level, rather than at the individual level, is that that allows the team to decide how the team will be most productive. If the team can be most productive by having one of its members sit out for a day, the team is free to make that decision.

Allowing individuals to have slack time is a counterintuitive way to maximize throughput, but at the end of the day, what matters to the organization is the total output from each team, not the output from each individual. If the team is effectively optimizing for team productivity, the organization shouldn't care about what's happening at the individual level.

Key Principle: Model Key Agile Behaviors

Effective leaders embody the behaviors they want to see from the people they lead. Those behaviors should include:

- *Develop a growth mindset*—commit to continuous improvement at both the personal and organizational levels.

- *Inspect and Adapt*—constantly reflect, learn from experience, and apply the learnings.
- *Decriminalize mistakes*—model the approach of accepting each mistake as an opportunity to learn.
- *Fix the system, not the individual*—when problems occur, look for the flaw in the system rather than blame the individual.
- *Commit to high quality*—use your actions to communicate a clear commitment to high quality.
- *Tighten feedback loops*—be responsive to your teams, even if they shouldn't need it because you've clearly expressed your Commander's Intent.

Suggested Leadership Actions

Inspect

Review your own performance as a leader:

- Are you treating your Agile teams as black boxes, managing to their performance in meeting their commitments rather than managing details?
- Have you expressed your "Commander's Intent" clearly? Can your teams express a vivid, current definition of success for their work? Can they work for a few weeks without your involvement, if necessary?
- Are you communicating priorities to your teams clearly?
- Do you stay focused on your team's throughput rather than their apparent level of activity?

Adapt

- Ask your teams to conduct a 360-degree review of your leadership performance according to the "Inspect" criteria above. Welcome your teams' feedback in a way that models learning from mistakes.
- Make a prioritized list of personal leadership self-improvement actions based on the results of your self-evaluation and your team's input.

Additional Resources

U.S. Marine Corps Staff. 1989. *Warfighting: The U.S. Marine Corp Book of Strategy*. New York : Currency Doubleday, 1989.

DeMarco, Tom. 2002. *Slack: Getting Past Burnout, Busywork, and the Myth of Total Efficiency*. s.l. : Broadway Books, 2002.

Maxwell, John C. 2007. *The 21 Irrefutable Laws of Leadership*. Nashville, Tennessee : Thomas Nelson, 2007. In a sea of books on management, this book truly focuses on leadership.

CHAPTER FIFTEEN

More Effective Agile Organizational Culture

More effective leadership will establish a more effective organizational culture. This chapter describes the organizational attributes that support more effective use of Agile practices.

Key Principle: Decriminalize Mistakes

As I've mentioned, Agile development depends on the use of *Inspect and Adapt.* Inspect and Adapt is a learning cycle that depends on making mistakes, learning from them, and improving. In Cynefin terms, Complicated projects depend on making small numbers of calculated mistakes, and Complex projects depend on making large numbers of calculated mistakes. It is thus essential that an effective organization decriminalize errors so that they are visible, examined, and ultimately beneficial to the organization, rather than hidden, shameful, and ultimately harmful to the organization.

	Accidental	Calculated
Repeated	System learning (coach teams to learn from mistakes)	Necessary for success on *Complex* problems
One Time	Individual learning (coach individuals to learn from mistakes)	Necessary for success on *Complicated* problems

Figure 15-2
Types of mistakes—a taxonomy of decriminalized mistakes.

As Jez Humble says, "In a complex adaptive system, failure is inevitable. When accidents happen, human error is the starting point of a blameless post-mortem." (Building and Scaling High Performing Technology Organizations, October 26, 2018). Some organizations such as as Etsy publicize and *celebrate* mistakes—the focus of the celebration is based on the idea that, "We're happy we made this mistake, because otherwise we never would have learned about *X*."

Psychological Safety

Decriminalizing mistakes is important, among other reasons, because it contributes to teams' feelings of psychological safety. A two-year research project conducted by Google's People Operations (HR) found that five factors contributed to team effectiveness at Google.

1 Psychological Safety
Team members feel safe to take risks and be vulnerable in front of each other.

2 Dependability
Team members get things done on time and meet Google's high bar for excellence.

3 Structure & Clarity
Team members have clear roles, plans, and goals.

4 Meaning
Work is personally important to team members.

5 Impact
Team members think their work matters and creates change.

Figure 15-3

The most important contributor to successful teams at Google is psychological safety.

Google's research found that, by far, the most important influence on team effectiveness was psychological safety, which they defined as, "Can we take risks on this team without feeling insecure or embarrassed?" Google described psychological safety as the underpinning of the other four factors. They found that:

> *"Individuals on teams with higher psychological safety are less likely to leave Google, they're more likely to harness the power of diverse ideas from their teammates, they bring in more revenue, and they're rated as effective twice as often by executives."*
> *(Rozovsky, 2015)*

Google's research is consistent with prior research by Ron Westrum (Westrum, 2005; Schuh, 2001). Westrum developed a "Three Cultures Model" of organizational cultures. He described the three cultures as pathological, bureaucratic, and generative. The attributes of these cultures are shown in Table 15-1.

Table 15-1 Attributes of Different Cultures in Westrum's Three Cultures Model

Pathological	Bureaucratic	Generative
Power oriented	Rule oriented	Performance oriented
Low cooperation	Modest cooperation	High cooperation
Messengers shot	Messengers neglected	Messengers trained
Responsibilities shirked	Narrow responsibilities	Risks are shared
Interdepartmental bridging discouraged	Interdepartmental bridging tolerated	Interdepartmental bridging encouraged
Failure → scapegoating	Failure → justice	Failure → inquiry
Novelty crushed	Novelty → problems	Novelty implemented

Westrum found that generative cultures are more effective than pathological and bureaucratic cultures—they perform beyond expectations, demonstrate higher flexibility (agility), and show better safety records.

Pathological organizations are characterized by suppression of bad news. Generative organizations publish bad news internally, and, through subsequent inquiry, they leverage the bad news into improvements. Westrum's work reinforces the importance of decriminalizing mistakes.

A Systems View of Organizational Capacity

An effective organization views itself as having a particular amount of capacity for software development work. This capacity is a function of individual productivity, team productivity, staff additions and losses, and gradual, measured productivity improvements over time. An effective organization measures this capacity and makes plans based on its measured performance history—typically based on each team's velocity, an empirical approach that's based on historical data. This approach contrasts with a more visceral approach in which an organization bases its plans on the expectation of future heroics (i.e., "insert miracle here").

The difference in approaches to self-assessed capacity for technical work comes into play in project-portfolio planning and in setting project deadlines. If the organization views its own capacity clearly, it will distribute work and assign deadlines that can be met by the teams. If the organization bases its plans on the assumption of abrupt increases in capacity, it will overload its teams and set up the teams and the overall organization for failure.

As discussed in Chapter 7, "More Effective Agile Projects," aggressive views of organizational capacity—and the schedule pressure that ensues—give rise to several unintended, ultimately destructive consequences:

- Teams aren't able to meet their commitments (sprint goals), which in turn means the organization isn't able to meet its commitments.
- Because teams aren't able to meet their commitments, team members do not feel a sense of mastery over their work and their motivation suffers.

- Excessive loading on teams competes with the growth mindset, which undermines the ability of the team and organization to improve over time.
- Excessive loading also results in burnt-out teams, higher turnover, and reduced capacity.

As I wrote in *Rapid Development* more than 20 years ago, the attempt by leaders to apply schedule pressure to their teams most often has the effect of sending teams into full-scale, counter-productive schedule panic—even when the leaders perceive themselves as applying only a tiny amount of pressure (McConnell, 1996). In Agile development today, the pressure focuses as much on functionality as on schedule, but the fundamental unhealthy dynamic is the same.

A healthy organization does not expect its individual teams or the overall organization to demonstrate abrupt changes in capacity, and it makes its plans based on its empirical performance.

The Role of the Organization in Supporting More Effective Agile

Some of the attributes that support successful teams are under the teams' control; many are controlled at the organizational level.

Agile teams cannot be successful if their organizations undermine their efforts. Organizations do this by blaming teams for mistakes, not supporting the teams' autonomy, not adequately communicating the teams' purposes, and not allowing for growth of the teams over time. Of course, this is not unique to Agile teams; it's true of teams in general.

Teams can be most successful if their organizations support them by establishing a blame-free culture organization-wide, staffing the teams with the full skill set needed, loading the teams with appropriate workloads, regularly communicating the teams' purposes, and supporting the teams' growth over time.

Depending on where you are in your Agile journey, other leaders in your organization might need to take this journey with you. If you refer back to the Agile boundary you drew in Chapter 2 ("What's Really Different About Agile?"), you can identify those other leaders and make plans for how to work with them.

Suggested Leadership Actions

Inspect

- Reflect on your reactions to teams' mistakes over the past few weeks or months. Would your teams interpret your reaction as decriminalizing mistakes and emphasizing the opportunity to learn from them?
- Interview your team members to assess their level of psychological safety. Can they take risks without feeling insecure or embarrassed?
- Perform a gap analysis between your organization and the generative culture in Westrum's model.
- Review your organization's approach to assigning workloads to teams. Are you setting expectations based on observed empirical capacity for work?

Adapt

- Make a personal resolution to decriminalize mistakes in your interactions with your teams.
- Communicate to your teams that you expect them to work at a sustainable pace that allows for learning and growth. Ask them to let you know if schedule expectations are preventing that.
- Make a plan to close the gaps identified in your gap analysis of Westrum's Three Cultures Model.
- Make a plan for how to bring other leaders in your organization along with you on your Agile journey.

Additional Resources

Rozovsky, Julia. 2015. The five keys to a successful Google team. [Online] November 17, 2015. [Cited: November 25, 2018.] https://rework.withgoogle.com/blog/five-keys-to-a-successful-google-team/.

A Typology of Organisational Cultures. Westrum, Ron. 2005. January 2005, Quality and Safety in Health Care, pp. 22-27.

Forsgren, Nicole, et al. 2018. *Accelerate: The Science of Lean Software and DevOps: Building and Scaling High Performing Technology Organizations.* Portland, OR : IT Revolution, 2018. This book contains a discussion of Westrum's organizational culture model applied to IT organizations.

CHAPTER SIXTEEN

More Effective Individuals and Interactions

The Agile Manifesto stated that Agile values individuals and interactions over processes and tools. But Agile to date has focused much more extensively on processes than individuals, and its focus on individuals has been limited to the interactions around certain structured collaborations.

The Potential of Focusing on Individuals

Maximizing individual effectiveness should be the cornerstone of any program intended to increase organizational effectiveness.

Researchers for decades have found that productivity among different individuals with similar levels of experience varies by at least a factor of 10 (McConnell, 2011). They have also found that differences in productivity among teams working in the same industries also varies by at least a factor of 10 (McConnell, 2019).

To some degree differences in personal effectiveness are probably born, not made, but to some degree they are made. Netflix's cloud architect, Adrian Cockroft, was once asked where he got his amazing people. He told the Fortune 500 leader, "I hired them from you!" (Forsgren, 2018). The point, of course, is that good performers don't become good performers overnight. They develop over time, which means an organization that wants to be effective has the opportunity to supports its staff in that development.

Supporting your staff's development is synergistic in numerous respects. The first and foremost reason to support staff development is because it increases staff members' ability to contribute to your organization. There's also synergy between the Inspect and Adapt growth mindset at the project level and a personal growth mindset at the professional development level. Finally, supporting staff development taps into the motivational power of *Mastery*.

As Forsgren, Humble, and Kim report in their far-reaching study of high-performing technology organizations:

> *"In today's fast-moving and competitive world, the best thing you can do for your products, your company, and your people is to institute a culture of experimentation and learning, and invest in the technical and management capabilities that enable it."*
> *(Forsgren, 2018)*

Forsgren, Humble, and Kim also reported that a climate for learning was one of the three factors that were highly correlated with software delivery performance.

More Effective Individuals

An organization that wants to be a more effective software organization will support its software staff by ensuring that their professional development experiences allow them to achieve higher levels of mastery.

Most software professionals' career progression can be described as lily-pad hopping, project-by-project, from one technology to another or from one methodology to another. Professional experience of any kind is valuable, but this pattern usually amounts more to treading water than to progressing along a course that builds expertise and capability over time.

The organization that wants to develop effective individuals will provide clear guidance about how to progress from junior engineer to senior engineer, how to move from development into management, how to grow from technical lead to architect, and so on.

The absence of defined career paths represents a significant lost opportunity for both the professionals and their organizations. To the organization, it represents an opportunity cost of lesser contribution from its staff than is possible with a powerful professional development program.

To the individual, it represents a lower level of personal development, and also a lower level of motivation, than is possible.

Construx's Career Pathing Program

Twenty years ago my company and I recognized that career pathing for software professionals was poorly defined and poorly supported, so we developed a detailed Professional Development Ladder (PDL) to provide both overall direction and detailed support for professional development of software staff. We have continued to maintain, update, and evolve the PDL since then, and we make many of the PDL materials freely available for software professionals and their organizations to use.

Construx's PDL supports long-term career pathing for a variety of software staff, including developers, testers, Scrum Masters, Product Owners, architects, business analysts, technical managers, and other common software positions. The PDL provides direction and structure while still allowing the interests of individuals to guide their specific career paths.

The PDL is comprised of four building blocks:

- Standards-based software development knowledge areas, such as requirements, design, test, quality, management, and so on
- Defined capability levels, such as introductory, competence, and leadership
- Professional development activities—including training, reading, and defined experience—needed to attain capability in each knowledge area
- Role-specific career paths, built using the knowledge areas, capability levels, and professional development activities described above

The Heart of the PDL: The Professional Development Matrix

The heart of Construx's Professional Development Ladder is an 11x3 Professional Development Matrix (PDM) that is produced when the 11 knowledge areas and 3 capability levels are combined. This is illustrated graphically in Figure 16-1.

	Knowledge Area										
Capability Level	Configuration Management	Construction	Design	Foundations	Maintenance	Management	Models and Methods	Process	Quality	Requirements	Testing
Introductory	●	●	●	●	●	●	●	●	●	●	●
Competence		●									●
Leadership											

Figure 16-1
The 11x3 Professional Development Matrix (PDM).

The Professional Development Matrix appears simple, but it is deceptively powerful. Career goals can be defined in terms of which boxes are checked in the matrix. Career progression can be defined by charting a path through highlighted sections of the matrix. Professional development activities can be defined in terms of which cells they support in the PDM.

The matrix arising from the combination of the 11 standards-based knowledge areas and the 3 defined capability levels provides a framework for career development that is simultaneously highly structured and highly flexible and customizable. Most important, it offers each software professional a clear path toward steadily increasing levels of mastery.

More Effective Interactions

While every team can improve if individuals improve their software development capabilities, many teams struggle more because of poor interactions. Agile development forces collaboration, so productive interactions are arguably more important in Agile development than they were in Sequential development. After working with leaders at many companies over the past 20 years, I believe the following interaction soft skills are most helpful to Agile team members.

Personality Types

Sales staff might intuitively understand that different people communicate differently and adapt their communications appropriately. Technical staff often need explicit instruction and encouragement to adapt their communication style to suit their audience.

A study of personality types helps technical staff understand that different people emphasize different kinds of factors in their decision making (e.g., data vs. people's feelings). They express themselves differently, and they react differently under stress. Labeling the variations, seeing how the variations apply to others, and self-assessing is often an eye-opening experience for technical staff members.

I find the Social Styles model to be an especially useful tool for understanding personality types (Mulqueen, 2014). DISC, Myers Briggs, and Color Codes are similar and are also useful.

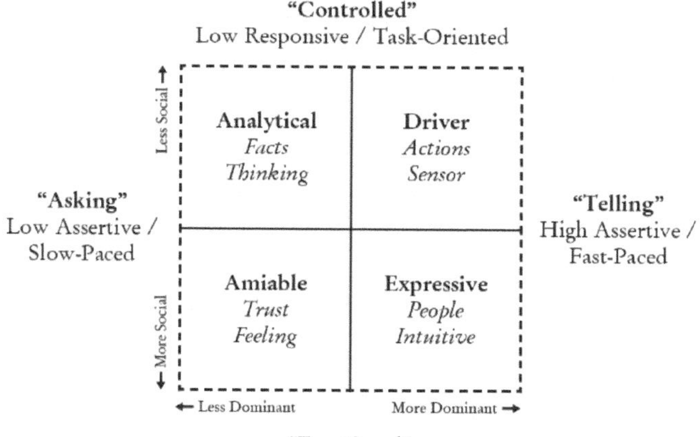

Figure 16-1

The outline of the Social Style model.

The value of appreciating differences in social styles is most obvious in improving interactions among different types of staff. Technical staff tend to be on the Analytical side, sales staff tend to be Expressive, and management tend to be Drivers. (These are all generalizations with numerous exceptions, of course.) Learning about social styles can help technical staff communicate more effectively with sales, it can help them do a better job of managing up in the organization, and it can help improve communications among different personality types within a team.

Emotional Intelligence

If you've ever seen two developers engage in an email flame war over technical minutia, you've seen evidence of the need for greater emotional intelligence on software teams.

For leaders, the value of emotional intelligence has been well-documented.

Daniel Goleman reported in the Harvard Business Review that 90% of the difference between star performers and average performers can be attributed to EQ (Goleman, 2004).

A study of 500 executive search candidates found that EQ was a significantly better predictor of placement success than intelligence or experience (Cherniss, 1999).

Technical contributors can benefit from increasing awareness of their own emotional states, awareness of emotional states in others, improving emotional self-regulation, and managing relationships with others.

I find the Yale Center for Emotional Intelligence's RULER Model to be a useful resource in this area (Yale Center for Emotional Intelligence). RULER stands for:

- Recognizing emotions in self and others
- Understanding the causes and consequences of emotions
- Labeling emotions accurately
- Expressing emotions appropriately
- Regulating emotions effectively.

The RULER model was originally developed for work with adolescents and was subsequently adapted for use with adults, especially adults working in groups.

Stages of Team Development

Although the Tuckman model of group development is almost a cliché in management circles, because software work is so often performed in teams, and because teams in many organizations change often, it's useful for team members to understand Tuckman's four phases: forming, storming, norming, and performing.

I've found that teams that are in the forming or storming phases are relieved to learn that what they're experiencing is normal, and that realization helps them move toward norming and performing more quickly.

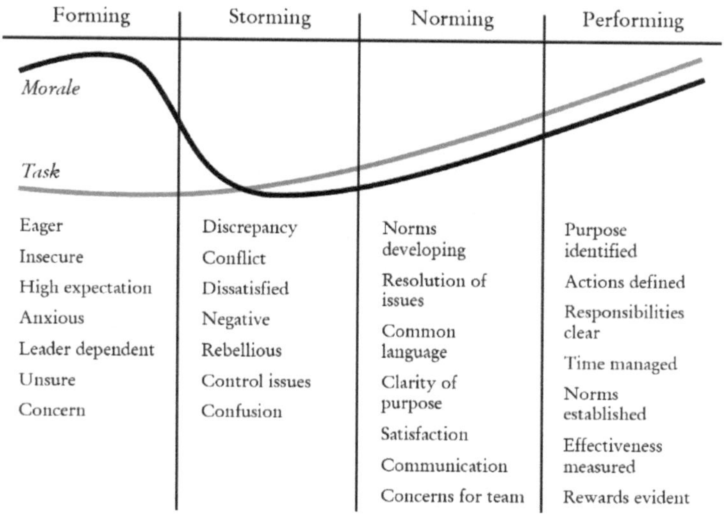

Forming	Storming	Norming	Performing
Eager	Discrepancy	Norms developing	Purpose identified
Insecure	Conflict	Resolution of issues	Actions defined
High expectation	Dissatisfied	Common language	Responsibilities clear
Anxious	Negative	Clarity of purpose	Time managed
Leader dependent	Rebellious	Satisfaction	Norms established
Unsure	Control issues	Communication	Effectiveness measured
Concern	Confusion	Concerns for team	Rewards evident

Morale
Task

Figure 16-1
The Tuckman Model's stages of team formation.

Crucial Conversations

Structured approaches can provide good support for people who don't have an intuitive sense of how to perform a task. The Crucial Conversations approach to having difficult conversations is an effective model for communicating when, "stakes are high, opinions vary, and emotions run strong" (Patterson, 2002).

Streamlined Decision-Making Models

Software teams need to make numerous decisions about requirements priorities, design approaches, work assignments, process changes—the list is endless. Knowing a few team-oriented decision-making models is useful. I have had success using streamlined decision-making practices including thumb voting, fist of five, dot voting, and decision leader decides.

Presentations to Executive and Other Communication Skills

Understanding the different personality types provides useful foundation for improved communication in general and better presentations to executives. Identifying the executive's personality type, understanding the executive's decision-making style, and anticipating how the executive is likely to react under stress can all help prepare for a successful presentation.

Conducting Effective Meetings

In many organizations meetings are a huge time killer, and many meetings are run ineffectively.

One of the benefits of Scrum is that Scrum's standard meetings are well-structured. The meeting roles, purpose, and basic agenda are all defined by Scrum, and that helps to keep the meetings on track and make good use of time.

For nonstandard meetings, it's useful to provide guidance in conducting meetings effectively. At a minimum this should include standard advice such as have a clear purpose for the meeting, set clearly defined expectations about what decision or other deliverable the meeting will produce, err on the side of scheduling the meeting to be shorter rather than longer, invite only people to the meeting who are necessary to support the meeting's deliverable, and so on. A good resource in this area is *How to Make Meetings Work* (Doyle, 1993).

Win-win Mindset for Interactions

Developing a mindset that focuses on how to help others be successful creates a virtuous dynamic within a team. The best model I know for this is Rotary International's Four-Way Test (The Four Way Test):

- Is it the truth?
- Is it fair to all concerned?
- Will it build goodwill and better friendships?
- Will it be beneficial to all concerned?

Any decision or interaction that passes the Four Way Test is likely to lead to a stronger team overall.

General Personal Interaction Skills

Any person can benefit from periodically reviewing their general personal interaction skills. Dale Carnegie's *How to Win Friends and Influence People* is as good a guide to effective interactions as it was when it was first published almost 100 years ago (Carnegie, 1936).

Suggested Leadership Actions

Inspect

- Reflect on your organization's approach to maximizing individual capability. Does the approach include ongoing development after each person is hired?
- Interview your staff. How important are well-defined opportunities for professional growth to them? How satisfied are they with the support they're receiving from the organization?
- Review the non-Agile-related interactions in your organization. How effectively does your staff conduct meetings, communicate to executives, and demonstrate other soft skills?
- Reflect on the conflicts you see within your teams, technical or otherwise. How would you score the emotional intelligence level (EQ) of your staff?

Adapt

- Through the use of Construx's PDL (or some other approach), ensure that each person on your staff has a defined program for professional growth that is meaningful to them.
- Create a plan for improving the interpersonal skills of the people on your teams, including learning about personality types, preparing for difficult conversations, communicating upwards and sideways in the organization, resolving conflict, and developing win-win outcomes.

Additional Resources

Lencioni, Patrick. 2002. *The Five Dysfunctions of a Team.* San Francisco, California : Jossey-Bass, 2002.

Maxwell, John C. 2007. *The 21 Irrefutable Laws of Leadership.* Nashville, Tennessee : Thomas Nelson, 2007.

Fisher, Roger and William Ury. 2011. *Getting to Yes: Negotiating Agreement Without Giving In, 3rd Ed.* New York : Penguin Books, 2011. This is the classic text on achieving win-win outcomes.

McConnell, Steve and Jenny Stuart. 2018. Career Pathing for Software Professionals. [Online] 2018. https://www.construx.com/whitepapers.

McConnell, Steve. 2004. *Professional Software Development.* Boston, Massachusetts : Addison-Wesley, 2004.

Patterson, Kerry, et al. 2002. *Crucial Conversations: Tools for talking when the stakes are high.* New York : McGraw-Hill, 2002.

Doyle, Michael and David Strauss. 1993. *How to Make Meetings Work!* New York : Jove Books, 1993.

The Four Way Test. About the Four Way Test. *The Four Way Test.* [Online] [Cited: January 12, 2019.] http://thefourwaytest.com/history-of-the-four-way-test/.

CHAPTER SEVENTEEN

More Effective Distributed Agile Teams

In more than 20 years of working with companies that have established geographically distributed development teams, we have seen only a small number of examples in which productivity was comparable to a team that was co-located. We have never seen an example where the distributed team's productivity was better than a co-located team's.

I have not seen any indication that geographically distributed Agile teams will ever be as effective as co-located teams. However, distributed teams are a fact of life for most large companies today, so the objective is often to make distributed teams work as well as possible.

Key Principle: Tighten Feedback Loops

One principle of effective software development is to tighten feedback loops as much as possible. Many of the details in this book can be inferred from that principle. Why do we want a Product Owner within the Agile team? To tighten the feedback loops related to requirements. Why do we have cross-functional teams in general? To tighten the feedback loop needed for decision making. Why do we want to define and deliver requirements in small batches? To tighten the feedback loop from requirements definition to executable, demonstrable software. Why do we perform test-first development? To tighten the feedback loop between code and test.

Geographically distributed teams have the effect of loosening feedback loops. That slows decision making, increases error rates, increases rework, reduces throughput, and ultimately delays projects. Any communication that can't occur face to face inserts more potential for miscommunication, which loosens the feedback loop. Time zone differences insert delayed responses, which also loosen the feedback loop. Work tends to be done in larger batches before being sent offshore, such as during the time an onshore Product Owner visits the offshore team to support face-to-face communication. That again loosens the feedback loops.

We work with a company at which the offshore team was significantly underperforming the onshore team. When we brought some of the offshore individuals onshore, their productivity increased dramatically for the short time they were working onshore, but it fell again when they returned home. This was not because of the individuals involved—the communications gap caused by 12,000 miles of separation made it impossible for the offshore team to perform effectively.

Loose feedback loops are the biggest problem I see with distributed teams. These appear in a number of forms, all of which I'm inclined to call classic mistakes:

- Development at one location; test at another
- Product ownership at one location; development at another
- Work on shared functionality that's split 50/50 across two sites

None of these configurations work well—each of them creates a situation in which people who need to communicate with one another frequently are delayed in their communications.

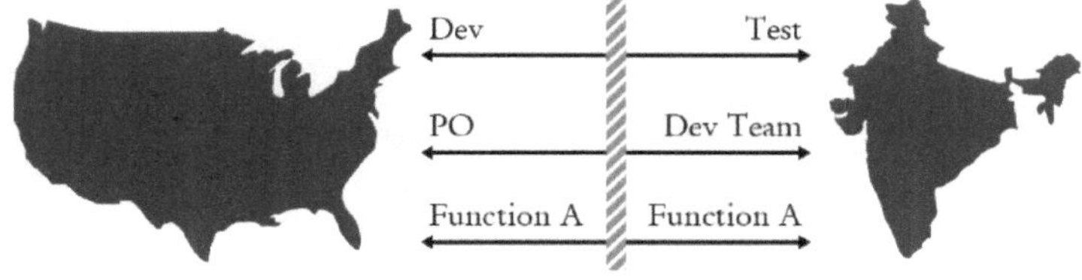

Figure 17-1
Examples of how not to allocate responsibilities across a distributed team.

The best practice in this area is to establish teams that can operate as autonomously as possible at each location. In software terms, think of the teams as having high cohesion and loose coupling.

It is also not an accident that the best practice for distributed teams is exactly the same as the best practice for Agile teams in general: establish self-directed cross-functional teams that have both the ability and the authority to make binding decisions at the local level.

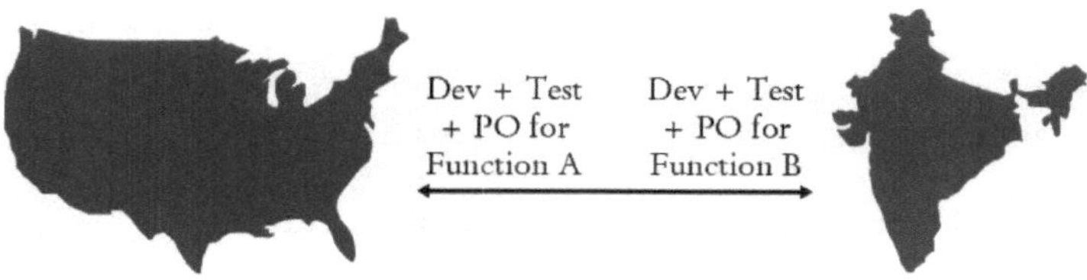

Figure 17-2
Example of a better way to allocate responsibilities across a distributed team.

Toward More Effective Distributed Agile Teams

In addition to tightening feedback loops, to make distributed teams as effective as possible you'll need to apply some of the principles that have already been discussed:

- Leverage autonomy, mastery, and purpose.
- Treat Agile teams as black boxes.
- Maintain high quality.
- Inspect and adapt.

In the short term, you can leverage these principles in the following ways.

Leverage Autonomy, Mastery, and Purpose

Some companies have teams that are evenly distributed across multiple sites, with each site having equal status. More commonly, companies that have multiple sites tend to create status discrepancies among their sites. Uneven status arises from sites being onshore vs. offshore, in-house vs. outsourced, parent company vs. acquired company, and main site vs. satellite sites. Companies allocate different kinds of work to their secondary sites, including allocating less important work to the secondary site and allowing those sites less latitude.

The differences in status and lower autonomy limits each site's motivation. I have found that secondary teams tend to be self-aware and candid about their status and level of responsibility. Managers who manage secondary teams frequently report that their teams ask for more autonomy and self-direction.

Managers also frequently report that secondary teams ask for opportunities to grow (mastery) and want to understand the bigger picture of the work they're doing (purpose).

Organizations that want to be successful with multi-site development, Agile or otherwise, should find ways to provide each location with work it can perform autonomously, and it should find ways to allow each site to grow professionally. They should also actively communicate why the work is important to the organization or the world at large.

Treat Agile Teams as Black Boxes

As with co-located teams, the management discipline of treating teams as black boxes supports managers acting more as leaders who set direction than as managers who are overly concerned with details. Manage inputs to your teams and outputs from your teams. Avoid focusing on the details of how your teams perform their work.

Maintain High Quality

The Agile discipline of keeping the software close to potentially releasable at all times helps to prevent teams at different geographies from diverging too much from one another.

Part of treating each team as a black box is assuring that the output that comes out of the box is high quality. The practice of keeping a code base at a potentially releasable level of quality is a high-discipline practice that even co-located teams struggle with.

Teams' natural tendency when they are distributed is to converge to a potentially releasable state less often. This is a mistake. Geographically distributed teams are exposed to a greater risk of going in different directions without realizing it, which means, for sake of risk management, that they should converge more often rather than less. To ensure they're converging effectively, distributed teams should pay special attention to their Definition of Done.

The effort required to keep the software at a potentially releasable level of quality highlights the costs of geographic distribution. If a distributed team finds that it's spending an inordinate amount of time in its frequent convergences to a potentially releasable level of quality, the solution is not to converge less often. That increases the risk that the team won't be able to converge at all! The solution is to modify practices to streamline the work required to converge reliably and frequently. In some cases, highlighting the convergence effort might lead to a decision to reduce the number of development sites.

Inspect and Adapt

Developing with geographically distributed teams is difficult, and the challenges will vary based on how many sites you have, where the sites are located, your software's architecture, how the work is allocated across sites, and the capabilities of the specific teams and individuals at each location.

For geographic distribution to work, teams must engage in regular retrospectives to candidly assess what's working, what's taking more time that it should, and whether issues related to working in a distributed team are causing problems or inefficiencies. The organization should also support system-level retrospectives that focus specifically on streamlining issues related to multi-site development.

The teams must then use those insights to make changes that address the difficulties they're identifying—and the teams must be empowered to make those changes. If they are not empowered, the organization risks low effectiveness from geographically distributed development.

Poor execution of distributed development can demotivate staff both at primary and secondary sites, leading to lower morale and higher turnover.

Many organizations—perhaps even most organizations—fail to achieve the objectives that led them to establish geographically distributed teams. You have to do a lot of things right to be successful with distributed teams, and this is not an area where you should take shortcuts.

Key Principle: Fix the System, Not the Individual

Geographically distributed development increases miscommunication, which in turn increase errors. Geographically distributed teams can count on spending a higher percentage of their time fixing defects than a co-located team would—because of both increased defect counts and increased defect-resolution times caused by distance between the teams. The increased error rates tend to increase stress, which increases the tendency to point fingers and assign blame.

If the organization wants to be successful with a geographically distributed team, it's important to emphasize the principle of decriminalizing errors. Treat errors as *system problems* rather than as personnel problems. The following question is appropriate: What is it about our system that allowed this error to occur? This is a good practice in general, and it's especially important in a geographically distributed environment.

Other Considerations

If you experience inefficiencies with your distributed teams because they are not able to make decisions locally, you should ask whether you are also experiencing similar challenges with your teams at your primary sites. It's possible that you are experiencing similar inefficiencies—they're just less visible because it's easier for the primary-site team to compensate for their lack of autonomy by working with people who are geographically closer to them.

Suggested Leadership Actions

Inspect

- How tight are the feedback loops with your distributed teams? Are you committing any of the classic mistakes listed in this chapter?
- Are your teams organized in such a way that each team can have Autonomy, Mastery, and Purpose?
- Are your distributed teams highly disciplined about converging to a potentially releasable level of quality often—*at least as often* as they would if they were co-located?
- Have you systematized your distributed teams' use of Inspect and Adapt so that they can learn how to work more effectively in their challenging configuration?

Adapt

- Reorganize your teams, if necessary, to tighten feedback loops.
- Make a plan for supporting your distributed teams in having Autonomy, Mastery, and Purpose.
- Communicate the importance of maintaining a potentially releasable level of quality at all times to your teams, and make sure they are using an appropriate Definition of Done.
- Empower your teams to make changes based on the findings of their retrospectives.

Additional Resources

Stuart, Jenny, et al. "Succeeding with Geographically Distributed Scrum," Construx White Paper, March 2018.

Stuart, Jenny, et al. "Ten Pitfalls of Enterprise Agile Adoption," Construx White Paper, July 2018.

CHAPTER EIGHTEEN

More Effective Agile Predictability

Decades ago, Tom Gilb asked the question, "Do you want predictability, or do you want control?" (Gilb, 1988). With little fanfare, Agile has caused a shift in many organizations' answer to that question. Sequential development tended to define a fixed feature set and then estimate the schedule—the focus was on *predicting* the schedule. Agile development tends to define a fixed schedule and then define the most valuable functionality that can be delivered in that time frame—the focus is on *controlling* the feature set.

Much of the Agile literature has focused on software development for markets that prioritize timeliness above predictability—consumer-oriented mobile applications, games, SaaS applications, Spotify, Netflix, Etsy, and so on. But what do you do if your customers still want predictability?

What if your organization still needs to deliver a specific feature set *and* it still needs to know how long it will take to deliver that feature set? Or what if you just want to get an idea of approximately how much functionality can be delivered in approximately how much time as an aid to optimizing the combination of functionality and schedule?

Agile has focused most often on feature set control, but Agile practices also provide excellent support for predictability, if appropriate practices are selected.

Predictability at Different Points in the Release Cycle

Agile-specific estimation practices are not available in the very early days of a project. Prior to populating the product backlog, the practices used for early-in-the-project estimates will be the same regardless of whether the project will later be conducted as Sequential or Agile (McConnell, 2006). It is not until the team begins working in sprints that the distinction between Agile and Sequential becomes relevant.

Figure 18-1 shows the point in the project at which Agile-specific estimation practices become relevant, expressed in terms of software's Cone of Uncertainty.

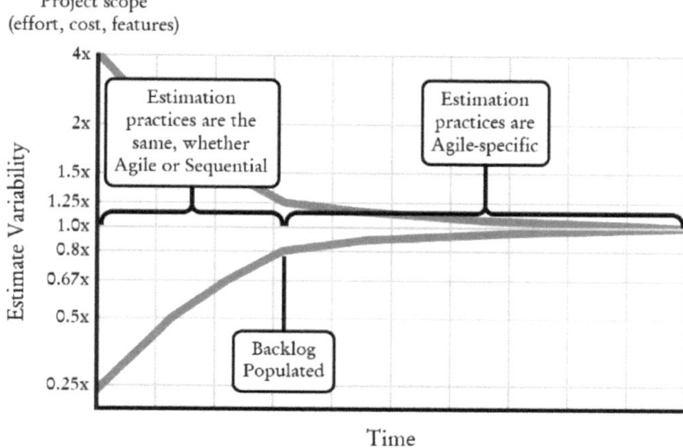

Figure 18-1

Estimation practices in terms of the Cone of Uncertainty. Agile-specific practices come into play after the backlog has been populated. Adapted from (McConnell, 2006).

There is an exception to this reasoning, which is that if you want a combination of predictability and control, rather than pure predictability, Agile practices come into play slightly earlier.

Kinds of Predictability

The following sections describe different approaches to predictability, and their interaction with control.

Strict predictability of cost and schedule. Sometimes you need to predict the cost and schedule for an exact feature set. Maybe you're replicating an exact set of functionality on a new platform. Maybe you're developing a specific set of functionality for a hardware device that has already been built. Maybe you're developing software under a non-Agile contract. These scenarios are all about prediction and don't involve much control. They are not the most common cases, but they do come up from time to time.

Strict predictability of features. Sometimes you need to predict the exact features that will be available at a fixed date with a fixed budget. This is a variation of the first scenario, and the practices used to support it will be similar.

Loose predictability. Sometimes you need to predict the feasibility of an approximate combination of functionality, cost, and schedule. None of the parameters is strictly fixed; each has at least a little flexibility. The need for this kind of predictability is common during budgeting when you're trying to assess whether there's a business case for developing functionality in a general area. It's also common to see it in practice once a project is underway. This kind of predictability can be accomplished through an iterative process that involves prediction combined with control.

The next two sections describe what's required to achieve strict predictability. The considerations involved in achieving strict predictability are also relevant to the loose predictability scenarios.

Strict Predictability of Cost and Schedule

If you need predictability about cost and schedule with an exact, fixed feature set, predictability comes into play after the exact feature set has been defined—which is usually 10-30% of the way into a release cycle.

The key Agile practices needed to support strict predictability are

- Populating the product backlog up front
- Assignment of story points

- Computation of velocity
- Completion of work in short iterations

Predictability Support: Populating the Product Backlog Up Front

The team that needs strict predictability will need to populate the product backlog with their release's full set of stories up front—that is, adopt a more Sequential approach to populating the backlog.

They don't need to elaborate stories as fully as they would in a full Sequential approach. But they do need to elaborate them enough to be able to assign story points to each backlog item, which is more than they would elaborate them up front in a typical Agile approach.

Predictability Support: Story-Pointing the Product Backlog Up Front

On Agile projects that aren't focused on predictability (strict or otherwise), teams assign story points on a just-in-time basis. This is a side effect of not refining themes and epics into stories until 1–2 sprints ahead of when they'll be implemented. Themes, epics, and other large backlog items are too large to support story-point assignments that are useful for strict predictability. Projects that need predictability need to decompose large backlog items into stories that are small enough to be assigned story points up front.

I'll provide more details about how to do that later in this chapter.

Predictability Support: Computing Velocity

The most common use of velocity is for sprint planning, one sprint at a time. An equally valuable use of velocity is to support predictability. If a team has been working at a sustainable pace and completing 50 story points per sprint for the past 3 sprints (an average velocity of 50), the team can use its average velocity to predict when it will deliver the total amount of functionality.

Suppose your company is planning a release that's 12 months out and consists of 1,250 story points. A 12-month schedule allows 26 biweekly sprints. The team works for 8 weeks (4 sprints) and sees an average velocity of 50 story points per sprint. At that time it's valid to predict that the team will require 1,250/50 = 25 sprints to complete the planned work. The team can likely deliver that feature set in its one-year timeframe.

There are a few ifs, ands, or buts on this statement. The stories that are used to calibrate the team's velocity need to be 100% complete—they must fully meet a rigorous Definition of Done. Also, the team can't be accumulating technical debt that it will need to pay off later in the release cycle, because that will drag down its velocity in later sprints. The projection of velocity needs to account for vacation and holiday schedules. Plans need to account for any work still needed after Definition of Done, such as User Acceptance Test, System Test, and so on. The velocity must also account for the sprint-to-sprint variability shown by the team (more on that later). But compared to traditional Sequential project estimation, the ability of a team to produce an empirically based calibration of its productivity early into a release cycle—and to use that to predict a completion date—is a powerful capability.

After the initial forecast, monitoring ongoing progress against the prediction is handled organically, in the normal flow of work. The team uses a release burndown to track the number of story points completed each sprint. If the team's velocity begins to change from its initial average of 50, it can inform stakeholders and adjust plans accordingly.

Predictability Support: Short Iterations

Velocity amounts to a calibration of the team's productivity. Velocity is computed on a per sprint basis, so the shorter the sprints are, the more often you can update a team's velocity. Compared to Sequential development in which complete-lifecycle iterations could take quarters or years—and therefore require quarters or years to fully calibrate a team's velocity or productivity—short iterations allow a team's velocity to be calibrated within only a couple of months.

Predictability Support: Small Stories

Typical story-point scales use the Fibonacci numbers from 1 to 13. For general use (not in support of predictability), some teams will use additional values such as 21, 40 and 100 (round numbers) or 21, 34, 55, 89 (Fibonacci numbers) to represent themes, epics, and larger backlog items.

For the sake of supporting strict predictability, stories should be decomposed so that they fit onto the scale of 1–13, and teams should take care to apply the story points proportionately. A story that's assigned 5 story points should be about 5/3 as large as a story that's assigned 3 story points. This allows a team to perform meaningful numeric operations on story points. A team can compare story points of different stories numerically. It can add the story points, and the sum of the story points will be arithmetically meaningful.

Numbers like 21, 40 and 100 are not meant to be used in the same way. They are more metaphorical than numeric and they are not intended as pure predictions of the sizes of those stories. A story that's assigned 40 points is not necessarily seen as being 5 times as large as a story that's assigned 8 points. It's just seen as "big." From a strict predictability point of view, it is not mathematically legitimate to add up the points of stories that have been assigned values of 40 or 100. Consequently, if your goal is strict predictability, larger stories should be decomposed so that they fit on the 1–13 scale. (If you're combining predictability and control it can be legitimate to add up the larger numbers. More on that later.)

Even if a team *intends* its assignments of 21, 40 or 100 to be used as literal numbers and to be used computationally, estimates based on those numbers will be error-prone, not due to any software-specific factor but due to the general limitations of human judgment (McConnell, 2006). When you hear a team disputing whether a backlog item is a 40 or a 100, you realize there's a lot of potential error in the prediction no matter which number they choose!

If a team confines itself to a scale of 1–13 and requires that all backlog items be decomposed into stories small enough to fit onto that scale, the potential for error is limited and the team can take advantage of a statistical property called the Law of Large Numbers.

The Law of Large Numbers, in general terms, says that when you estimate one large quantity, that estimate will contain some error and the error will be either all on the high side or all on the low side. If you break that large quantity into multiple smaller quantities and estimate each of those smaller quantities individually, each of those individual estimates will also contain error, but some of the errors will be on the high side, some will be on the low side, and the errors will tend to cancel each other out, to some degree. In other words, the aggregate error for a decomposed estimate is usually lower than the aggregate error for a non-decomposed estimate.

In story-point assignments, this means that when a team assigns a set of stories values of, say, 5, some of those stories will actually have a value more like a soft 5 or a 3; some will have values more like a hard 5 or an 8; and the highs and lows will cancel each other out to some degree. Any individual story that was defined as a 5 could turn out to be 1 or 13 or any number in between, but the average of all the stories that were defined as 5s should turn out to be pretty close to 5.

Predictability problems arise when the team allows itself to estimate using larger values like 21, 40, and 100.

The first problem is related to the fact that the Law of Large Numbers depends on having *a lot* of numbers—enough for the highs and lows to cancel each other out. Any given product backlog will have enough stories with values of 1, 2, 3, 5, 8, and 13 for the Law of Large Numbers to work. But backlogs inherently have fewer epics, themes, and other large items with assigned values of 21, 40, and 100. Because there's less opportunity for high and low errors to cancel out, the overall error will tend to be higher.

The second problem is that the error associated with each individual large item will be larger because the base point number is larger. A story estimated as a 3 that's really a 5 undermines the overall estimate by only 2 points. But a story estimated as a 100 that's really a 167 (which is the same percentage error) undermines the estimate by 67 points.

When you combine these two factors, you can end up with a significant amount of error arising from the use of large story point values.

A third problem with assigning larger story-point values is separate from the Law of Large Numbers. If a team allows estimates of 21, 40 and 100 for themes and epics, the teams typically re-estimate those items when they decompose epics into stories. It would not be uncommon for an epic that had been estimated to be 40 story points to be decomposed into stories that add up to a number much higher than 40. You can't count on highs and lows to cancel out when estimating epics because, when humans estimate large quantities, we have a systemic tendency to underestimate (McConnell, 2006). This is a problem if you need strict predictability. (If you're OK with a combination of predictability and control it's a different story.)

The bottom line: From a strict predictability point of view, is that the highest accuracy and lowest risk estimate is created when the team decomposes the product backlog into stories that are small enough to be story-pointed using a scale of 1–13. Teams can choose to use larger numbers if they want to, but the risk to predictability will increase if they do.

Predictability Support: Accounting for Variability in Velocity

Any team's velocity will show variability from sprint to sprint. A team that averages 50 story points per sprint might actually have completed sprints of 42, 51, 53, and 54 story points. This suggests that using the team's velocity to predict a long-range outcome includes some variability or risk.

The team with those four sprints showed a standard deviation of 5.5 story points vs. its average of 50. You can use a confidence interval based on the number of sprints completed and the standard deviation of those sprints' velocities to estimate risk to the team's ultimate, whole-project velocity. You can update that as the team gains more experience.

Table 18-2 shows an example. Based on a 90% confidence interval, the team is showing that it will require a total of 23–27 sprints to complete the work of 1,250 story points. The team has demonstrated a low standard deviation, which produces a narrow range of possible outcomes—a good level of predictability. There's a risk of a one-week overrun, but it's most likely that the team will complete within its one-year timeline.

Because of how confidence intervals are calculated, the more sprints the team completes, the more the range will tighten up and the better the predictability will be.[6]

---

[6] A confidence interval is a measure of how confident you can be that the observed mean (average) is close to the actual mean. In this example, a 90% confidence interval says you can be 90% confident that the actual mean will be between 45.5 and 54.5.

Table 18-2 Example of Using a 90% Confidence Interval to Predict a Range of Schedule Outcomes

Story points completed		200
Story points remaining		1,050
Number of sprints completed ("n")		4
Average velocity to date ("AVG")		50
Standard deviation ("σ")		5.5
Standard error ("SE")	$= \sigma/n^{1/2}$	2.75
90% confidence Z value ("Z")†		1.65
Margin of error ("ME")	= Z*SE	4.5
High velocity	= AVG + ME	54.5
Low velocity	= AVG - ME	45.5
Nominal sprints remaining (total sprints)		21 (25)
High-velocity sprints remaining		19 (23)
Low-velocity sprints remaining		23 (27)

† This value is a look-up value from a statistical reference table.

If a team's standard deviation were higher, predictability would be reduced. If a second team had shown per-sprint velocities of 34, 67, 38, and 61, that would still be an average velocity of 50, but the standard deviation would be 16.4 rather than 5.5. If you plug those numbers into the formulas in Table 18-2, the formulas predict that the second team will need a total of 21–33 sprints to complete its work. That wide range caused by the team's high standard deviation does not support a very good level of predictability; it suggests that the second team itself is not operating predictably.

Working with a team's velocity is never an exercise in pure predictability because one of the goals is to help teams achieve stability in their velocities. As the team works to improve its practices, its variability should come down and predictability should improve.

Strict Predictability of Feature Set

If you have a fixed cost and schedule and need to predict exactly what features can be delivered for that fixed cost and schedule, the approach is similar to what was just described. Here's how the approach plays out across the key Agile practices involved.

Creation of the product backlog

The backlog must be fully populated just as it was in the approach used to achieve strict predictability of cost and schedule.

If the team defines and refines stories that add up to more story points than the team has time for, some of that definition and refinement work will be wasted. The more the team can perform its backlog population work from high priority to low priority, the less waste there will be.

Computation of velocity, used to predict functionality

Velocity is used similarly to how it is used in the strict predictability of cost and schedule scenario. However, instead of using velocity to predict an end date, velocity is used to predict the amount of functionality that can be delivered. You use the math to show how variability transfers into the feature set rather than into the cost and schedule.

Using the same example as above—with the first team whose goal is to produce 1,250 story points in one year (26 sprints)—the last few rows in Table 18-2 show how velocity can be used to predict ranges in feature set outcomes.

Table 18-3 Example of Using a 90% Confidence Interval to Predict a Range of Feature-Set Outcomes

Story points completed		200
Sprints remaining		22
Number of sprints completed ("n")		4
Average velocity to date ("AVG")		50
Standard deviation ("σ")		5.5
Standard error ("SE")	$= \sigma/n^{1/2}$	2.75
90% confidence Z value ("Z")		1.65
Margin of error ("ME")	= Z*SE	4.5
High velocity	= AVG + ME	54.5
Low velocity	= AVG - ME	45.5
Nominal story-point capacity remaining (total one-year capacity)		1,100 (1,300)
Low story-point capacity remaining		1,001 (1,201)
High story-point capacity remaining		1,199 (1,399)

Based on a 90% confidence interval, the team should deliver a total of 1,201–1,399 story points, and chances are good that the team will be able to meet its goal of 1,250 total points.

With the track record of the second team that had high variability, the range of total story point outcomes would be 1,003–1,597, which does not support good predictability.

Assignment of story points and completion of work in short iterations

Assignment of story points on the scale of 1–13 works the same way for strict predictions of feature sets as it does for strict predictions of cost and schedule. The same guidelines apply to use of short iterations too.

Looser Approaches to Predictability

The discussion so far has been based on a pure predictability approach. At some point in the project, the organization wants to be able to predict the exact combination of cost, schedule, and functionality that will ultimately be delivered—without changing any of them very much. The need for this level of predictability is common in some industries, and comes up only occasionally in others.

The more common need I see is for a looser level of predictability that allows for ongoing manipulation of cost, schedule, functionality, or all three, to achieve an acceptable outcome. As I've written previously, many times the role of estimation is not to make a pin-point prediction, but to gain a general sense of whether this general type of work can be completed in that general time frame (McConnell, 2000). This is not really "prediction," because the entity you're predicting keeps changing. It's really a combination of prediction and control. Regardless of how it's characterized, it can meet the organizational need for "predictability," it can be an effective way to conduct a software project, and Agile practices provide good support for this loose predictability.

Loose Predictability During Top-Level Budget Planning

Some Agile coaches recommend avoiding the values of 21, 40, and 100 and larger Fibonacci numbers for detailed estimation but using them for top-level budget planning. From a strict prediction point of view, using those numbers in that way is not valid for reasons already described. From a looser pragmatic point of view, using numbers in that way can serve a useful purpose. The organization just needs to be aligned on what those larger numbers mean.

Using a Verbal Scale Instead of Large Numbers

One approach for budget planning is to avoid large numbers and use non-numeric terms such as "large epic," "medium epic," and "small epic." That allows a team to make statements like, "We have 850 story points of functionality that have been decomposed to the story-point level. We have an additional 5 large epics, 11 medium epics, and 4 small epics." Management can decide whether that provides enough information to go forward or whether additional work should be invested in decomposing the epics to clarify the scope of work.

Large Numbers as Proxies for Risk

Alternatively, you can assign numeric values to epics (or other large items), recognizing that each use of a larger number adds a little bit more risk to your predictability. Review the ratio of points from detailed stories vs. points from epics. If 10% of your points are from epics, there's not much risk to your overall predictability. If 50% of the points are from epics, risk to predictability is higher. Depending on how important predictability is to you, that might matter, or it might not.

Large Numbers as Detailed Budgets

Another approach to estimating epics and other large items is to use numeric estimates and treat those numbers as budgets for detailed work in each area. For example, if you're using a Fibonacci scale and the team estimates an epic as 55 story points, from that point forward you treat the 55 story points as the allowable budget for that epic.

From a strict predictability point of view, you would refine the epic into whatever stories best supported the epic. You would stay as true to the spirit of the epic as possible and let the story points turn out however they turn out. Underestimation of large quantities being what it is, that would likely result in stories that add up to more than 55 story points.

With the epic-as-detailed-budget approach, when your team refines the epic into detailed stories, it is not allowed to exceed the 55 story point budget for that epic. Your team will need to prioritize its more detailed stories and choose those that provide the highest business value within the 55 point budget.

This kind of approach is common in other kinds of work. If you do a kitchen remodel you'll have an total budget for the remodel, and you'll have a detailed budget for cabinets, appliances, countertops, hardware, and so on. The detailed budget approach works equally well for software teams. It provides the organization with a feeling of predictability—one that is achieved through the combination of predictability and control.

From time to time the team will blow it's budget—it won't be able to deliver the essence of the intended functionality within its 55 story point budget. That will force a conversation with the business about the priority of the work, and whether it's worth extending the budget. This kind of dialog is healthy, and story point assignments facilitate it. But it is an example of how this approach does not provide the same level of predictability that the strict approaches do—which might be acceptable or even preferable if your organization values incremental course corrections more than pure predictability.

Predicting Delivery Dates for a Combination of Core Feature Set and Additional Features

Some organizations don't need predictability of 100% of a feature set. They need assurance that they can deliver a core feature set within a particular time frame, and they can be opportunistic about the features they deliver beyond that.

If the team we've been using as an example needs to deliver a core feature set of 1,000 story points, it can predict that it will complete that core feature set after about 20 sprints (40 weeks). That leaves a capacity of about 300 story points (6 sprints). The organization can make long-range commitments to its customers about the core features, while still leaving some capacity available to deliver just-in-time functionality.

Predictability and the Agile Boundary

Most organizations can use the looser approaches described in this chapter most of the time and meet their business purposes. Some organizations have higher needs for predictability and need the stricter approaches.

Some Agile pundits will complain that elaborating the product backlog to the degree needed to support fine-grain story-pointing up front is "not Agile." These are the same pundits who complain that if your whole organization isn't Agile no individual part of your organization can be Agile. But the goal isn't simply to be Agile (at least not if you care about the topic of this chapter). The goal is to use Agile practices and other practices to support the objectives and strategies of your business.

The "Agile boundary" concept described in Chapter 2 ("What's Really Different About Agile?) is useful here. As Shown in Figure 18-1, for sake of strict predictabilty some of the early activities will need to be approached more Sequentially, and after that the rest of the project can be conducted in a fully Agile way.

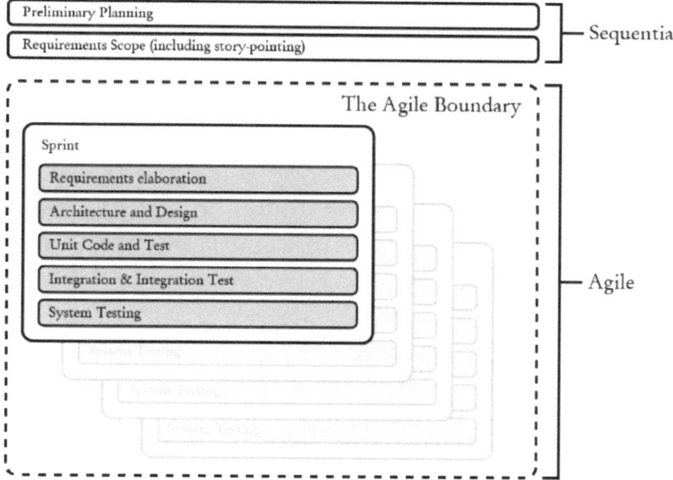

Figure 18-2

The concept of the Agile boundary helps to support long-range predictability—for organizations that need that.

The Agile boundary applies to external customers as much as it does to internal development organizations. We've worked with companies that have developed the ability to release software much more often than they do—they release less often because their customers have requested that. Their customers are on the other side of the Agile boundary.

Predictability and Flexibility

The discussion in this chapter has been focused on organizations that have a business need for long-range predictability. Agile practices provide excellent support for that objective.

The fact that an organization needs long-range predictability does not mean it will never change its plans. The organization that maps out 1,250 story points of functionality early in the year will sometimes decide to change course halfway through the year. *There is nothing wrong with that.* If the team is using Agile practices, it will be able to respond to the change in an organized and efficient way. Yes, some of the work on early requirements elaboration will be discarded, amounting to waste, but less work will be discarded than if the team had been using a Sequential approach that fully elaborated each requirement up front. Plus, the team will be able to change direction more easily because of the short-iteration structure of its work.

Other Considerations

Predictability and Cynefin

Fully defining a product backlog early in a release cycle depends on most of the work being in the Cynefin framework's Complicated domain. If the work is mostly Complex, it won't be possible to elaborate the work fully and reliably until it's done. Recall that a major focus of a project operating primarily in the Complex domain is conducting probes to determine the very nature of the problem that needs to be solved.

Strategies such as Barry Boehm's spiral model (Boehm, 1988) have been suggested to investigate projects that have significant Complex aspects and convert them to Complicated before diving into full-scale work. That can be a useful approach for an organization that values predictability. However, not every Complex problem can be converted to Complicated, and work on problems that are mostly Complex will never be very predictable. One valuable use of Cynefin is to examine aspects of a problem early to gain an understanding of the extent of Complex elements in the problem, and then to use that to assess what degree of predictability will be possible. If you see a project that has mostly Complex elements, ask whether predictability is even theoretically possible for that project.

Predictability and Agile Culture

Predictability can be a touchy subject for Agile teams. One failure mode we've seen with Agile adoptions is teams that refuse to provide estimates, even after their businesses describe sensible reasons for needing them. We've seen more than one Agile adoption shut down for this reason.

We've also seen instances of Agile pundits advising teams to avoid providing estimates and instead coach their whole organization into becoming more Agile so that estimates aren't needed. Aside from being instances of the tail trying to wag the dog, these examples amount to attempts by the development teams to dictate business strategy to the business.

One of the original values described in the Agile Manifesto is *customer collaboration*. If you are the customer and, rather than providing what you're asking for, your Agile teams are insisting that your business needs to redefine itself, you might suggest a renewed focus on that particular Agile value.

Suggested Leadership Actions

Inspect

- What is your business's need for flexibility vs. predictability?
- Does your business need strict predictability, or will looser predictability suffice?
- Do your teams understand that the goal of Agile development is to support the needs of the business and that sometimes the business needs predictability?
- Consider the practice of treating epics as budgets. How would that approach work on your teams?
- Assess each of the projects in your portfolio according to the Cynefin framework. Are your teams being asked to estimate work that is inherently Complex?

Adapt

- Talk with your teams about your business's need for predictability. Explain why it's important to your business (if it is).
- For each Complex project, assess whether the project can be converted to Complicated. For those that remain Complex, shift your focus from prediction to exploration.
- Ask your teams to refine their use of Agile practices to better support your business's need for predictability, including treating epics as budgets.

Additional Resources

McConnell, Steve. 2006. *Software Estimation: Demystifying the Black Art.* Redmond, Washington : Microsoft Press, 2006. This book is still the best book that I know of on software estimation on Sequential and Agile projects, especially for early-in-the-project estimation (before the Agile vs. Sequential distinction comes into play). Note that some of the discussion of requirements' role in estimation has been superceded by the progressive approach to requirements elaboration that's defined in *More Effective Agile.*

CHAPTER NINETEEN

More Effective Agile in Regulated Industries

The early Agile focus on flexibility at all costs created the impression that Agile practices were not well-suited for regulated industries such as life sciences, finance, and aerospace. The focus on "go full Agile or go home" reinforced the impression that Agile practices were not applicable for companies that could not see how to make their customers or their overall product development cycles fully Agile.

As Agile has matured, it turns out that Agile practices can be as useful and appropriate in regulated industries as they are anywhere else. It is certainly possible to practice Agile development in a way that will not meet the standards of regulated industries, but it's equally possible to practice Agile development in a way that does. In 2012, the FDA adopted AAMI TIR45:2012 ("Guidance on the use of AGILE practices in the development of medical device software") as a recognized standard. My company has been working for more than 10 years with numerous companies in FDA- and FAA-regulated environments to adopt Scrum and other Agile practices successfully.

How Agile in General Supports Work in Regulated Environments

In very general terms, the software-related requirements for work in regulated environments boil down to, "Document what you plan to do; do what you said you were going to do; and prove, with documentation, that you did it." Some environments add an additional requirement: "Provide extensive traceability to prove you did all that at a fine level of detail."

Agile practices don't make work in regulated environments more or less difficult. The documentation around the practices is the greater concern. The efficiency with which documentation can be produced is probably the most important consideration in adapting Agile practices for use in regulated environments.

Sequential practices support efficient creation of documentation in regulated environments. Agile's emphasis on incremental and just-in-time practices increases the number of times that documentation must be created or updated.

Table 19-1 summarizes how the Agile emphases affect compliance in regulated environments.

Table 19-1 How the Agile Emphases Come into Play in Regulated Environments

Agile Emphasis	Regulated Environment Implication
Short release cycles	No effect on compliance per se, but the cost of each release can be significant and might affect how often the organization chooses to release
End-to-end development work performed in small batches	No effect on compliance per se, but affects when documentation can be created
High-level up-front planning with just-in-time detailed planning	Plans must be documented, even just-in-time plans, and traceability can be required, depending on the type of regulation
High-level up-front planning with just-in-time detailed planning	Requirements must be documented, even just-in-time requirements; affects time that documentation is created
Emergent design	Design must be documented, even just-in-time design; affects time that documentation is created
Continuous testing, integrated into development	Supports compliance
Frequent structured collaboration	No effect on compliance
OODA as improvement model	Supports compliance as well as PDCA

At a conceptual level, several Agile practices provide support for the intent of regulations, which is to guarantee high-quality software:

- Definition of Done (which is created in a way that meets or exceeds regulatory requirements)
- Definition of Ready
- Software quality maintained at a potentially releasable level at all times
- Test development either preceding development of code or following immediately behind it
- Automated regression test use
- Regular Inspect and Adapt activities to improve product and process quality

How Scrum in Particular Supports Work in Regulated Environments

Regulations can be slow to be updated. The regulated environment requirements I described above were initially created decades ago, at a time when software development amounted to the Wild West. An organization could have been using practically any approach to develop software, and most of the approaches didn't work very well. Regulations are intended, in part, to avoid chaotic, *ad hoc* practices with unknown levels of efficacy.

US federal regulations do not generally require a specific software development approach or lifecycle. They require that organizations choose and define a model and document it, as described above.

Agile practices, especially Scrum, have been formalized and extensively documented (including in this book), which supports this requirement. If a team agrees to use Scrum and documents that it's using Scrum, as defined in a specific document, that contributes to creation of a defined process, which supports regulatory compliance.

Mapping Scrum onto Required Process Documentation

Regulations vary, and this section uses IEC 62304 (medical device software—software lifecycle processes) for sake of illustration.

IEC 62304 requires activities and documentation in these categories:

- Software development planning
- Requirements analysis
- Software architectural design
- Software detailed design
- Software unit implementation and verification
- Software integration and integration testing
- Software system testing
- Software release

As suggested by AAMI TIR45, these activities can be mapped onto an Agile lifecycle model, as shown in Figure Figure 19-1. This approach effectively divides the regulated Agile project into four layers:

- *The project layer*—the entire set of activities for a project. A project consists of one or more releases.
- *The release layer*—the activities needed to create a usable product. A release consists of one or more increments. (Certain regulatory environments impose significant requirements on releases—for example, the

requirement to be able to recreate an exact bit-wise image of any software that has ever been released for the life of the device—which makes releases rare.)

- *The increment layer*—activities needed to create useful functionality but not necessary a usable product. An increment consists of one or more stories.
- *The story layer*—activities needed to create a small, possibly incomplete, piece of functionality.

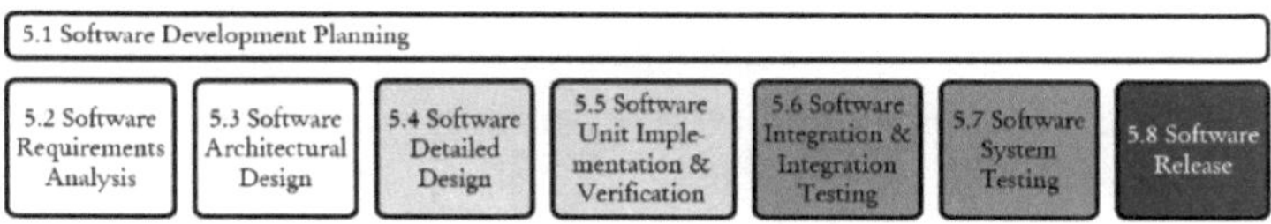

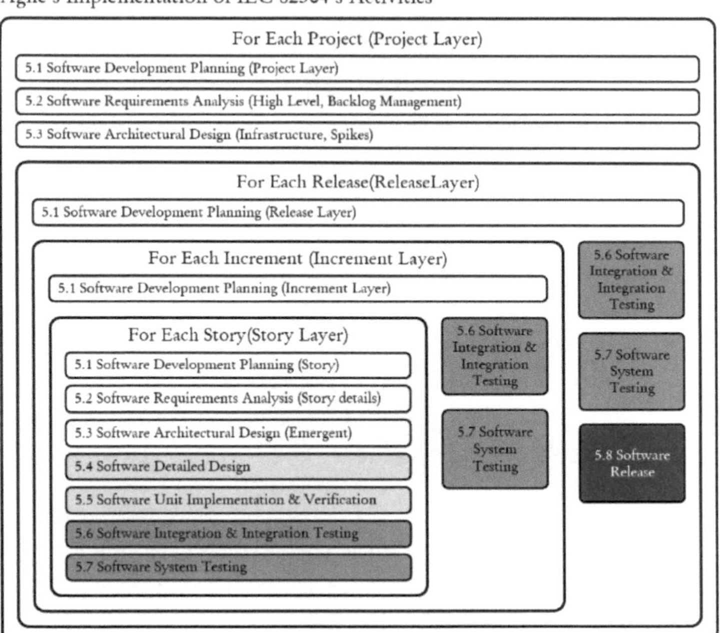

Figure 19-1

Mapping of example regulatory process documentation categories onto Scrum activities. Adapted from (AAMI, 2012).

In a Sequential approach, each activity would be performed mostly in a single phase. With an Agile approach, most activities are spread across layers.

In a nonregulated Agile approach, most activities would be documented informally. With a regulated Agile approach, the activities will be documented more formally.

Partly in support of generating documentation efficiently, the allocation of work across sprints will be adapted to meet regulatory requirements. Here is an approach that has been used successfully:

- Use the first sprint (or sprints) to define the general scope of the project, plan for release, and lay out architectural foundations.
- Conduct normal Scrum sprints, by the book. The Definition of Done includes as-built documentation for the sprint, including mapping each user story to code and test cases.
- In preparation for release, perform a documentation sprint that focuses on buttoning up documentation to meet regulatory requirements, including synchronizing requirements and design documentation with code and test outputs and running tests in a formal way that creates verification records.

There are variations on this approach that I'll discuss next.

The Agile Boundary for Regulated Systems

Cost of documentation is a considerable concern in development of regulated software, and it can be useful to apply the "Agile boundary" concept to software development activities. Consider the generic set of software activities:

- Planning
- Requirements
- Architecture
- Detailed design
- Unit implementation and verification (code and unit test)

- Integration and integration test
- Software system test

With no documentation requirements, you might find great value in applying a high degree of iteration from planning all the way through software system test. You might find value leaving requirements to be defined just in time, right before unit implementation begins.

With documentation requirements, however, you might decide that it's too costly to provide a high degree of iteration in requirements and it's more cost-effective to use a more Sequential approach. With that in mind, you might draw your Agile boundary after architecture and before software system test, as shown in Figure 19-2.

This suggests that you'll use a mostly Sequential approach for planning, requirements, and architecture; shift to a more incremental approach for the detailed implementation work; and then shift back to a Sequential approach for software system testing.

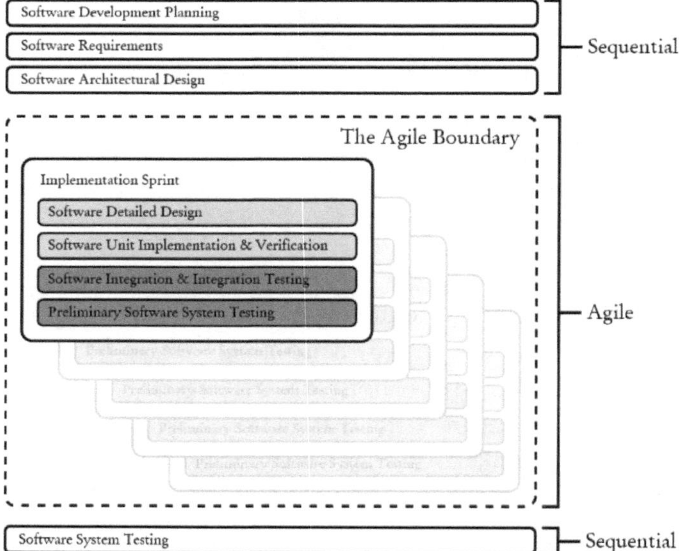

Figure 19-2

An example of where a development initiative in a regulated industry might draw their Agile boundary.

Some Agile pundits would complain that this approach is "Not really Agile," but the goal is not to be Agile. The goal is to use available software development practices to best support the business. When you factor in the cost of producing documentation, a combination of Sequential and Agile approaches sometimes works best in regulated environments.

Overall, an Agile implementation in a regulated industry will be more formal, more structured, and require more documentation than a nonregulated Agile implementation. Software teams in regulated industries will nonetheless benefit from Agile's shorter end-to-end unit development cycles, continuous testing, tighter feedback loops, frequent structured collaboration, and reduced waste due to a higher proportion of just-in-time planning—and possibly just-in-time requirements and design.

Other Considerations

In our work with companies in regulated industries, we have found that "regulatory requirements" do not always come from regulations. Sometimes they come from calcified organizational policies that have lagged behind regulations.

We worked with one life sciences company that enforced design traceability—being able to trace features through to the specific software modules affected. We analyzed which of the development process requirements were mandated by the FDA and which were required by the company's regulatory group. We were able to eliminate about one-third of the design documentation, which was not mandated by the FDA and which was essentially useless.

We have found requirements being treated as regulatory requirements that come from a company's experience with client audits rather than from a regulatory agency. We have also found that sometimes documentation requirements come from software capitalization rules rather than industry regulatory requirements.

Overall, I suggest that you be sure to understand the sources of your regulatory requirements. Have a discussion with your regulatory groups to understand which requirements are real regulatory requirements and which are the regulatory group's opinion about what is needed for clients or for financial practices. You can then make decisions about the necessity of carrying forward your company's historic documentation requirements into your current development efforts.

Suggested Leadership Actions

Inspect

- Investigate the sources of the regulatory requirements in your company. Which requirements arise from current regulations, and which arise from other sources?
- Determine where you are currently drawing the Agile boundary for software development activities in your organization. Is it drawn in the best location?
- Review your QA activities and when and where defects are found. Assess whether Agile practices would allow more defects to be found sooner.

Adapt

- Create a plan to redraw the Agile boundary for activities in your organization to better support your organization's goals, including the goal of cost-effective documentation.
- Based on your assessment of when and where defects are found, create a plan to shift your quality practices earlier.

Additional Resources

AAMI. 2012. *Guidance on the use of AGILE practices in the development of medical device software*. 2012. AAMI TIR45 2012. This is the definitive reference for Agile in regulated industries at this time.

Collyer, Keith and Jordi Manzano. 2013. Being agile while still being compliant: A practical approach for medical device manufacturers. [Online] March 5, 2013. This readable case study describes how one team met regulatory requirements using an Agile approach.

CHAPTER TWENTY

More Effective Agile Portfolio Management

Many organizations sequence their project portfolios quite informally. They use intuitive practices to decide which projects to start first and which to finish first.

These organizations do not realize just how much their informal approach to project portfolio management is costing them. If they did, they would literally choose to burn stacks of $100 bills before they would choose to manage their project portfolios by using seat-of-the-pants methods.

The gap in value between intuitive approaches to portfolio management and mathematically based approaches is wide, and Agile projects' shorter cycle times create even more opportunities to optimize the value delivered through a well-managed portfolio.

Weighted Shortest Job First

The primary tool for managing an Agile project portfolio is Weighted Shortest Job First (WSJF).

The concept of Weighted Shortest Job First comes from Don Reinertsen's work on lean product development (Reinertsen, 2009). In Agile development, it's primarily associated with SAFe, but the concept is broadly applicable regardless of whether an organization is using SAFe.

WSJF starts with an identification of the "cost of delay" (CoD) associated with each feature or story. CoD is a not-very-intuitive term that refers to the opportunity cost of *not* having a feature available. If a feature will save your business $50,000 per week once it goes online, the cost of delay is $50,000 per week. If the feature will generate $200,000 per week in revenue once it goes online, the cost of delay is $200,000 per week.

WSFJ is a heuristic for minimizing the cost of delay for a set of features. Suppose you have the features listed in Table 20-1.

Table 20-1 Example Set of Features with Information Needed to Calculate WSJF

Feature	Cost of Delay (CoD) (000s)	Development Duration (Weeks)	WSJF: CoD / Duration
Feature A	50	4	12.5
Feature B	75	2	37.5
Feature C	125	8	15.6
Feature D	25	1	25

According to the table, the initial total CoD is $275,000 per week (the sum of all the CoDs). Once you start delivering functionality, you stop incurring CoD for the functionality you've delivered.

The rule in WSJF is that you deliver the feature with the highest WSJF first. If multiple items have the same CoD, you do the shortest one first.

Suppose that we implemented the features strictly in order from largest CoD to smallest. A diagram of the CoD would look like Figure 20-1.

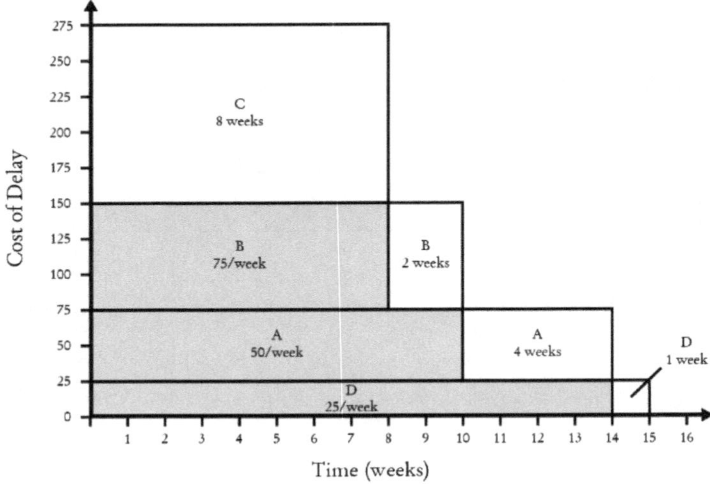

Figure 20-1

CoD for example features delivered in descending order of business value.

The white rectangles represent the feature that is currently in progress—work begins initially on Feature C (highest CoD), then on Feature B, then on A, and finally on D (lowest CoD).

CoD accumulates for each feature until it is completed. Total CoD is calculated as the total area occupied by the rectangles, shaded and unshaded. In this example, the total CoD is $2.825 million: 8 weeks times $125,000/week for Feature C, plus 10 weeks times $75,000/week for Feature B, and so on.

Figure 20-2 shows the features sequenced by descending WSJF—which is CoD divided by duration—rather than raw CoD. The dashed line shows the curve from the first chart.

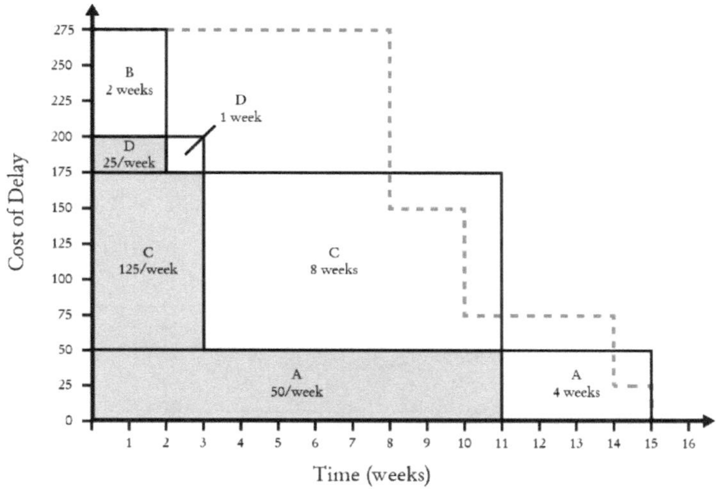

Figure 20-2
CoD for example features delivered in descending order of WSJF.

Visually, you can see that the total area in the rectangles when the features are delivered in this order is smaller than the area for the decreasing-CoD ordering. Mathematically, the total CoD with this sequencing works out to $2.35 million, a decrease in CoD (or increase in business value) of $0.475 million. This is an incredible increase in business value achieved simply by resequencing the order in which you deliver features!

A Much Worse Common Alternative to WSJF Sequencing

Sequencing based on Cost of Delay is common, even though WSJF is a demonstrably better way to sequence delivery. An even worse delivery order—and a common non-Agile one—is to level-load all four features on a budgeting cycle, beginning all four features at the beginning of the cycle and not delivering any of the features until the end of the cycle.

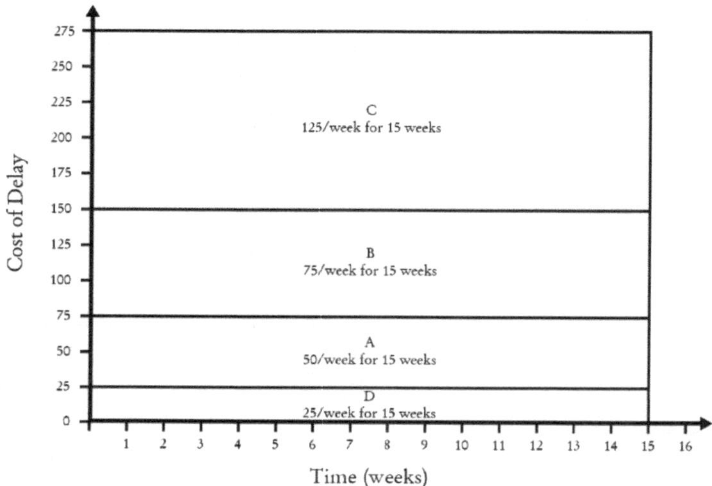

Figure 20-3

CoD for features delivered on a budget-cycle basis.

Total CoD for this approach is $4.125 million, which is far worse than either of the other approaches.

A mantra in Lean is "Stop starting, start finishing." The lost opportunity represented in this example would not be very visible in an organization using Sequential development on a quarterly or annual cadence. It becomes much more visible (and painful) when an organization moves to a weekly or biweekly cadence.

Applicability of WSJF

WSJF depends on calculation or estimation of cost of delay, which limits the technique to use on features that can have CoD attributed to them individually. As a practical matter, this limits use of WSJF to fairly large-grain "features," such as epics, themes, value streams, or entire projects. At that large-grain level, as you can see from the example, the business value obtained by using WSJF to sequence work easily justifies the effort needed to perform the WSJF analysis.

Other Considerations

T-Shirt Sizing

Described in Chapter 11, "More Effective Agile Requirements Prioritization," the T-shirt sizing approach can be used to plan at the portfolio level, and we have worked with companies that have done that successfully. However, if a company is able to calculate Cost of Delay for its initiatives, the significant business value available from using WSJF makes WSJF preferable.

Overuse of Leading-Edge Practices

Agile pundits might criticize this book as not representing the leading edge of Agile practices, but that is precisely the point—this book focuses on practices that have been proven to work, not on practices that someone, somewhere, got to work one time.

Experimenting with leading-edge practices (also known as speculative practices) is an important part of a comprehensive process improvement strategy—apply them to 5–10% of your project portfolio. Committing a larger portion of your project portfolio to speculative practices is a better way to end up as a poster child for the j-curve-hype-disillusionment cycle than it is to achieve more effective software teams.

Suggested Leadership Actions

Inspect

- Reflect on what size feature, requirement, or project would be large enough to support calculation of cost of delay in your organization. Would using CoD and WSJF improve your teams' feature-level planning or just project portfolio–level planning?
- Examine your current project portfolio using CoD and WSJF. Obtain CoD information from your business and development duration from your teams. Calculate overall CoD of your current prioritization. Calculate the WSJF order for your portfolio, and then calculate what your overall CoD would be if you resequenced your portfolio in WSJF order.

Adapt

- Sequence your project portfolio using WSJF.
- Consider applying WSJF to smaller-grain items such as epics.

Additional Resources

Reinertsen, Donald G. 2009. *The Principles of Product Development Flow: Second Generation Lean Product Development.* Redondo Beach, California : Celeritas Publishing, 2009.

Humble, Jez, et al. 2015. *Lean Enterprise: How High Performance Organizations Innovate at Scale.* Sebastopol, CA : O'Reilly Media, 2015. This book also discusses WSJF and is more readable than Reinertsen's book. It renames WSJF "CD3" (Cost of Delay Divided by Duration).

Tockey, Steve. 2005. *Return on Software: Maximizing the Return on Your Software Investment.* Boston : Addison-Wesley, 2005. This book contains a detailed discussion of economic decision making in an engineering context, including interesting discussions of decision making under risk and uncertainty.

CHAPTER TWENTY-ONE

More Effective Agile Process Improvement

How do you summarize effective Agile's approach to process in four words? My answer is, "*Fix systems, not individuals.*" I talked previously about decriminalizing mistakes, which is important. But decriminalizing mistakes does not mean ignoring them—it means coming together in an open, respectful, collaborative way to understand the factors that led to the mistake and changing them so that the mistake cannot happen again.

Much of this book has focused on the specifics of more effective Agile processes. This chapter focuses on a few specifics of Agile process *improvement*.

Scrum as a Process Improvement Baseline

Good Scrum implementations often repeat this mantra: "Scrum doesn't solve your problems, but it shines a bright light on them so that you can see what they are." Scrum has the ability to expose issues, including teams being starved for requirements, leadership not prioritizing requirements, leadership redirecting teams too often, and other similar issues.

If we go back to the days of Software Capability Maturity Model (SW-CMM), Level 2 was a defined, repeatable process. That established a baseline that allowed for measured improvements at higher levels in the SW-CMM. A high-fidelity Scrum implementation accomplishes the purpose. The Scrum team has a baseline process that it follows consistently. Regardless of how well it works, it establishes a baseline that supports the team improving from there.

Measurement

The story-point measurement known as velocity (described in Chapter 7, "More Effective Agile Projects) forms a backbone for process improvement work on Agile projects. Key metrics include:

- *Item velocity*—the rate at which work is completed
- *Scope velocity*—the rate at which scope is added to an ongoing project
- *Defect velocity*—the rates at which defects are found and fixed
- *Rework percentage (R%)*—the percentage of effort focused on rework vs. new development

Less effective Agile implementations sometimes treat measurement as the enemy. More effective Agile implementations use measurement to make process changes based on quantitative data rather than subjective opinion. As Dave Moore, former Director of Development at Microsoft used to say, "Get technical about your processes" (Moore, 1996).

Measuring velocity with story points sets up a team to measure the effect of process changes. If you have work occurring both onshore and offshore and you move the Product Owner from onshore to offshore, what happens to velocity? If velocity goes up over time, the change worked. If it goes down, the change should be reconsidered.

Short sprints provide frequent opportunities to experiment with process changes, track the results of changes, and build on the successful changes. Improvements accumulate rapidly with this approach. We have routinely seen teams double, triple, or even quadruple productivity through a disciplined tracking of story point–based velocity, candid retrospectives, and rigorous attention to each change's effect on velocity.

Measurement Cautions

Performance measurement can be loaded topic for software teams, so it's important to do it well.

Avoid Cross-Team Comparisons

Leaders often want to measure teams for sake of comparing their performance, and that's a natural desire. For numerous reasons, trying to measure team performance is an error-prone activity that is virtually impossible to do in a meaningful way in software (McConnell, 2016).

A more useful focus for measurement of software teams is process improvement, in which the focus of the measurement is helping each team improve relative to its own historical performance.

The Agile technique of story points doesn't support cross-team comparisons, because each team's implementation of story points is effectively unique. It's as though one team reports results in dollars, another in pounds, another in euros, another in yuan, and another in rupees. Comparing results across teams is not meaningful.

What Gets Measured, Gets Done

If you measure only one thing, people naturally optimize for that one thing. Be sure to include a balanced set of measures for people to optimize against. Specifically, if you're tracking velocity measures, be sure also to track quality measures so that teams don't optimize for velocity at the expense of quality.

Beware of Gaming of Measures

As you focus on process improvement, especially if you're focusing on productivity improvement, be sure that increases in velocity are due to increases in productivity, not due to changes in what work is being measured.

Different teams take different approaches to what kinds of work are assigned story points (which is one of many reasons that cross-team comparisons aren't valid). Some teams assign story points to defect correction work, and some don't. Some assign story points to spikes, some don't. Some story-point scales go to 8, some to 13, some to 20. Some of these variations work better than others, in my experience, but what never works is changing the kind of work that counts as story points instead of making genuine process improvements.

If you find a team that's gaming its measures, that's an opportunity to avoid criminalizing the mistake. Take a systems view of the behavior, and fix the system that's causing the problem. The intent of measurement is to support improvement, and according to the "Mastery" part of Autonomy, Mastery, and Purpose, teams generally want to improve. Measurement is a useful tool in service of improvement, so determine the system dynamic that is undermining the team's natural desire to improve. Is it excessive schedule pressure? Insufficient time for reflection and adaptation? Lack of permission to make process changes that would lead to improvement? This is an opportunity to reflect on your performance as a leader and assess the effect that's having on your teams.

Daily Kata

Toyota's manufacturing processes have provided a lot of inspiration for Agile development. The Toyota Production System is usually cited as the basis for Lean methodologies, for example.

Toyota Kata is a useful model for institutionalizing an Inspect and Adapt mindset. Coming from Japanese martial arts, the word "kata" refers to a form that's practiced individually or in groups for purpose of memorizing and improving the movement. Similarly, the Toyota Kata is a form that is intended to be practiced, resulting in improvement over time. The Toyota Kata consists of a four-step pattern, as shown in Figure 21-1.

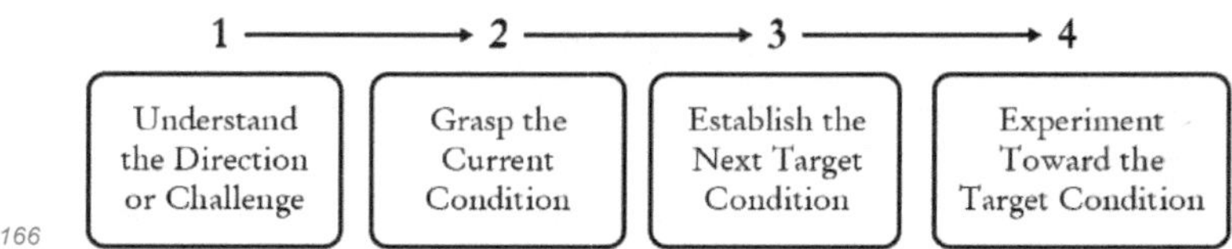

Figure 21-1
The Toyota Kata. What does this remind you of?

Step 1 is to understand the problem. Step 2 is to contextualize the problem in current conditions. Step 3 is to establish what you want to do in response to the problem. Step 4 is to implement your action—conceived as an "experiment"—and determine whether it moves you toward your desired result.

If you study these steps, you'll see that the Toyota Kata is essentially an OODA loop that is intended to be practiced every day until it becomes a habit. Everyone agrees with the idea of continuous improvement. A daily kata provides a way to institutionalize that focus.

Disciplined Mapping and Monitoring of Work in Progress

As organizations move beyond basic Scrum, it becomes useful to mix in Lean. Kanban is the Lean technique most often used to implement Lean's requirement to visualize and map work flow across a value stream.

Kanban emphasizes examining "work in progress" (WIP), defining how much WIP exists in a system at present, and then gradually imposing limits on WIP so as to expose delays that are limiting throughput.

In Lean terms, work is always in one of three categories:

- *Value*—work that immediately adds concrete value and that the customer is willing to pay for.
- *Necessary waste*—work that doesn't add value on its own but that is the supporting work necessary for adding value, such as testing, eating lunch, and so on.
- *Unnecessary waste*—work that doesn't add value, that hurts throughput, and that can be eliminated.

The function of WIP limits is to expose waiting time, which the largest source of waste on software projects. Examples of waiting time include:

- Waiting for completion of manual acceptance testing after code has been unit tested, integration tested, and checked in before the functionality can be deployed.
- Waiting for bugs detected by an independent testing organization to be fixed by development before the software can be deployed.
- Waiting for a code review before a story can be completed in a sprint.
- Waiting for a Product Owner at one location to refine a story before the Development Team at another location can begin implementing the story.
- Waiting for a team at one location to check in code that needs to be completed before a team at another location can proceed with its work.

One way or another, waiting time on software projects delays functionality from being released and, therefore, is always a form of waste.

When teams first map their work flows, they usually find that they have too much WIP—usually, far too much WIP!

A disciplined focus on WIP will highlight that improvements to throughput are rarely related to maximizing utilization of individual staff members. The desire to keep every staff member busy at all times more often creates WIP, which creates bottlenecks, which reduces throughput. A focus on WIP can be incredibly useful in helping an organization shift its focus from maximizing busy-ness to maximizing throughput.

A detailed discussion of Kanban and Lean is beyond the scope of this book. Further reading is suggested at the end of this chapter.

The Agile Retrospective

Inspect and Adapt is used end to end on Agile projects, and the retrospective meeting provides a focal point for that work.

On Scrum projects, the sprint retrospective is held at the end of the sprint, after the sprint review, prior to sprint planning for the next sprint.

The purpose of the retrospective is to inspect how the sprint went, generate improvement ideas, and create a plan for implementing improvements in the next sprint. The Scrum Master facilitates the meeting, and the whole Scrum team participates. Teams vary in their perspective on whether outside participants should be allowed to observe or participate. I believe that management and other outside parties should be allowed to review the improvement plans that emerge from the retrospective, but maximizing candor within the retrospective itself is more important than allowing outside observers.

The general flow of the meeting follows this sequence:

1. Set the stage.
2. Gather input; create a shared pool of information.
3. Generate insights; look for patterns; look for root causes; review the big picture.
4. Decide what to do; identify experiments to be conducted by the team; create an action plan.
5. Close the retrospective, including reviewing how the retrospective itself could be improved.

The focus of the retrospective can be on any areas that could improve performing during the next sprint, including

- Processes and practices
- Communication
- Environment
- Work products
- Tools

The retrospective is time-boxed. Two hours is a typical length for a 2-week sprint.

Current Scrum practice is to ensure that each retrospective results in at least one change being made in the next sprint. The effect of that change is reviewed at the next retrospective, and it is either retained or discontinued.

Inspect and Adapt

In addition to the formal retrospective, the Inspect and Adapt mentality should apply end to end on Agile projects. Scrum provides several structural opportunities for Inspect and Adapt to occur:

- Sprint review
- Sprint retrospective
- Sprint planning

- Any time a defect is discovered to have escaped beyond its sprint

Effective use of Inspect and Adapt depends on having some *impatience*. Teams that are patient with their problems end up living with them for a long time and not improving. Teams that insist on doing something about their problems can improve incredibly rapidly.

Effective use of Inspect and Adapt can also benefit from some structure and transparency. We've had success with teams putting proposed process changes into their product backlogs and prioritizing and planning process improvement work along with their other work. This helps avoid the failure mode of retrospective findings becoming "write-only" documents.

Suggested Leadership Actions

Inspect

- Investigate whether your teams have established a consistent Scrum practice, which forms a baseline against which you can measure.
- Review your team's attitudes toward measurement. Do your teams understand that measurement supports them in making changes that will ultimately improve the quality of their work lives?
- Review your team's performance in their sprint reviews, retrospectives, and sprint planning. Are they taking advantage of these opportunities to Inspect and Adapt?
- Map your work flow and look for delays. Assess how much waste you have in your delivery process due to unnecessary delays.

Adapt

- Begin measuring the effect of process changes by using story points.
- Insist that teams make consistent use of Inspect and Adapt during the relevant Scrum events.
- Proactively communicate to your teams that retrospectives are important and that you support your teams making changes immediately, in the next sprint, based their retrospectives.
- Institute a daily kata to institutionalize the Inspect and Adapt and OODA mindsets.
- Visualize your teams' work using Kanban, and look for delays.

Additional Resources

Derby, Esther and Diana Larsen. 2006. *Agile Retrospectives: Making Good Teams Great.* s.l. : Pragmatic Bookshelf, 2006.

Hammarberg, Marcus and Joakim Sunden. 2014. *Kanban in Action.* Shelter Island, NY : Manning Publications, 2014.

Oosterwal, Dantar P. 2010. *The Lean Machine: How Harley-Davidson Drove Top-Line Growth and Profitability with Revolutionary Lean Product Development.* New York, NY : AMACOM, 2010.

Poppendieck, Mary and Tom. 2006. *Implementing Lean Software Development.* s.l. : Addison-Wesley Professional, 2006.

Rother, Mike. 2010. *Toyota Kata: Managing People for Improvement, Adaptiveness and Superior Results.* s.l. : McGraw-Hill, 2010.

CHAPTER TWENTY-TWO

More Effective Agile Adoptions

Other parts of this book describe the specific Agile practices that make up the details of an Agile adoption. This chapter discusses adoption itself, a form of organizational change. Whether you're partway through an Agile adoption that's struggling or you're just beginning a new adoption, this chapter describes how to make your adoption successful.

General Change Approach

At the 20,000 foot view, the intuitive approach to Agile adoption seems straightforward:

Phase 1: Begin with a pilot team. Charter an initial team to trial an approach to Agile development in your organization. Work out the stumbling blocks at the single-team level.

Phase 2: Propagate Agile practices to one or more additional teams. Roll out Agile practices to additional teams, making use of lessons learned from the pilot team. Work out additional kinks, including inter-team issues.

Phase 3: Roll out Agile practices to the entire organization. Making use of lessons learned in Phase 1 and 2, roll out Agile practices to the remainder of the organization. Use the team members from Phase 1 and 2 as coaches for the remaining teams.

This is all logical and intuitive, and it even kind of works. But it omits important elements of support needed to support a successful rollout, and it overlooks a pivotal relationship between pilot teams and larger scale rollouts.

The Lippitt/Knoster Change Model

For anticipating kinds of support needed for a successful Agile adoption, I like a change model that is inspired by work originally created by Tim Knoster and extended by Mary Lippitt.

In the Lippitt/Knoster model, a successful organization change requires these elements:

- Vision
- Consensus
- Skills
- Resources
- Incentives
- Action plan

If all elements are present, a successful change occurs. If any of the elements is missing, however, the change will stumble. Figure 22-1 shows what happens when each of the elements is missing.

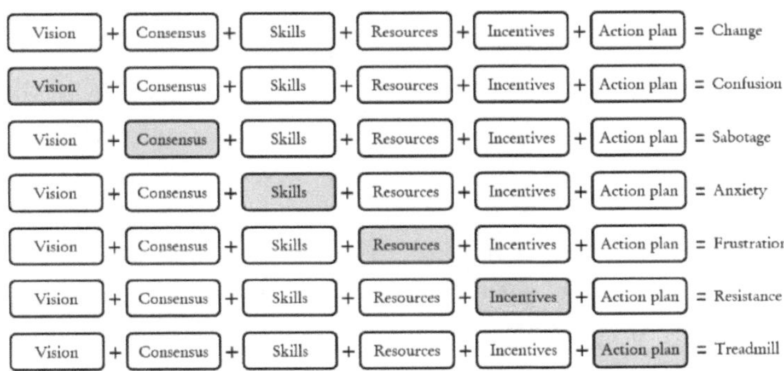

Figure 22-1

The Lippitt/Knoster change model describes required elements for change and the effects of missing elements.

The remainder of this section walks through these elements.

Vision

According to the Lippitt/Knoster model, a lack of vision leads to confusion. And this starts with the definition of Agile itself. As I described in Chapter 2, different people can have vastly different understandings of what "Agile" means. Without clear vision, one person will believe that "Agile adoption" refers to the whole business being redesigned to be more nimble. Another will believe it simply means implementing Scrum company-wide. Leadership needs to communicate a clear definition of "Agile."

Beyond that definition, the vision should include a *detailed articulation of the desired end state*. That articulation should include why the Agile adoption needs to occur, what the expected benefits are, how deep and widespread the adoption will be, and how will it affect each person individually—ideally not generically or by category, but one by one.

Pushing a change without clear vision will lead to the perception that "Leadership doesn't know what's doing."

Consensus

In the Lippitt/Knoster model, lack of consensus leads to sabotage, and my company has witnessed numerous examples of that. Variations of sabotage include "scrummerfall" (doing waterfall but renaming the practices using Scrum terms), Scrum-but (omitting necessary elements of Scrum), little or no energy exerted to overcome minor obstacles, and grumbling and passive resistance.

Leadership pushing a change without building consensus leads to the perception that "Leadership doesn't care about us."

Articulating a clear vision goes a long way toward building consensus, and communicating that actively, far more than you think you need to, is necessary.

True consensus building involves two-way communication: leaders describing the vision and being receptive to feedback about the vision. In a true consensus process, the vision might be affected. A leader needs to be open to the possibility of adjusting the vision—and being willing to do that is really just another instance of Inspect and Adapt.

Skills

You can't compel someone to do something they aren't capable of doing, and so trying to perform an Agile adoption without developing the necessary skills leads to anxiety. When leadership tries to push a change without building necessary skills, it creates the perception that "Leadership is unreasonable."

Building skills requires basic nuts-and-bolts professional development, including formal training in the classroom or online, discussion groups, reading clubs, lunch and learns, time to practice new techniques, internal coaching, external coaching, and mentoring.

Resources

One common dynamic we've seen in our work is management wanting to make a change and wondering why it's taking so long while their staff also wants to make the change but believes that management won't let them make the change. We refer to this as management and staff being in *violent agreement*—they just don't know it.

One cause of this dynamic is staff being asked to make a change without necessary resources—they necessarily will feel they are being prevented from making the change.

Bearing in mind that software development is intellectual, skills-based work, the kinds of resources needed for software change include access to training, access to coaching, and licenses to tools. Although it might not seem necessary, staff also needs explicit permission to work on the adoption and time explicitly approved for this work. Without that, day-to-day task focus will take precedence. Larger organizations usually need full-time staff driving the adoption.

Without adequate resources, staff perception will be that "Leadership doesn't really mean it."

Incentives

Without incentives, you can expect resistance. This is natural, because people don't want to make changes that are not in their self-interest. Most people feel that the comfort of the status quo is in their self-interest—any change requires justification.

This is another area in which a vividly articulated vision helps. The incentives don't have to be monetary, and they don't have to be tangible. Each individual needs to understand why the change matters to them, why it is in their personal self-interest. This is a lot of work and requires a lot of sustained communication. But without it, the perception will be that "Leadership is taking advantage of us."

Remember to consider Autonomy, Mastery, and Purpose. A high-fidelity Agile implementation will increase individuals' and teams' autonomy. The focus on empirically based planning and a growth mindset will support learning and mastery. The leadership style most appropriate to support Agile teams will regularly communicate purpose.

Action Plan

Without an action plan, the adoption will stall. Specific tasks need to be assigned to specific people, and timelines need to be established. The plan needs to be communicated to everyone involved, which, in an Agile adoption, is everyone. It's basic but often overlooked: If people don't know what to do to support the adoption, they aren't going to do it!

Pushing a adoption without an action plan leads to the perception that "Leadership is not committed to the change."

Most large organizations have initiated numerous change cycles, most of which never reach fruition. After experiencing a few of these cycles, many staff adopt the approach of keeping their heads down and hoping the change blows over before it affects them. Their organization's track record says there's a lot of merit to that approach.

Remember to incorporate Inspect and Adapt into the action plan. The change should be incremental and should involve improvements throughout the rollout based on regular retrospection and the application of lessons learned.

Propagating Change Through the Organization

The Lippitt/Knoster model is useful both for planning an Agile adoption and for diagnosing the causes of a stalled adoption.

There's another aspect to adoption that's not contained in that model, however, one related to problems in how organizations pilot Agile practices and how they then proceed to roll out the practices on a larger scale.

In contrast to the idealized rollout described at the beginning of this chapter, many organizations' rollouts look more like this:

- The organization commits to an Agile adoption.
- The initial pilot team succeeds.
- The second or third teams to adopt the changes stumble or fail—the teams fail outright, the team abandons the new practices and reverts to old practices, or no teams can be found that will follow the pilot team.

Why does this happen? You're probably familiar with Geoffrey Moore's "Crossing the Chasm" model as it applies to market adoption of new innovations (Moore, 1991). I've found that the same dynamic applies to adoption of innovations *within* organizations.

Moore's model was based on seminal work by Everett Rogers, described in his book *Diffusion of Innovation* (Rogers, 1995). Because this discussion doesn't depend on Moore's notion of the "Chasm," I'm going to concentrate on Rogers' description.

In Rogers' model, innovations are adopted from left to right across the categories of adopters shown in Figure 22-2.

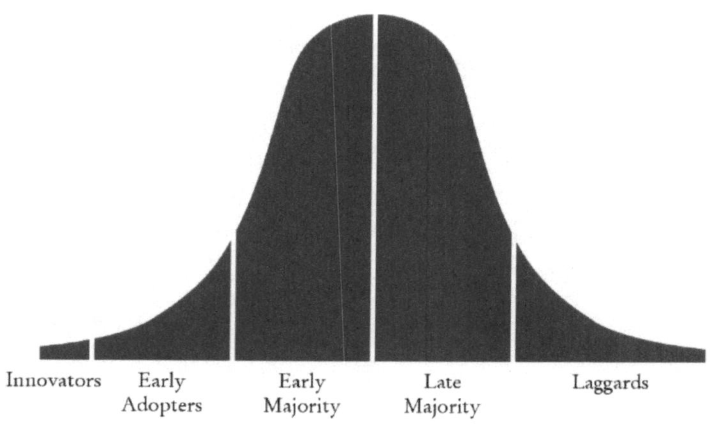

Figure 22-2
The innovation adoption sequence.

Each category of adopters displays certain attributes. The *Innovators* (the earliest adopters) are adventurous and eager to try new technologies or practices. They are attracted to novelty for the sake of novelty. They can cope with a high degree of uncertainty. They're highly risk-tolerant. They fail often, and they aren't bothered by that because they're so motivated by the prospect of being the first person to get something new to work. Because they fail often, they might not be respected by adopters in the other categories.

Early Adopters share some attributes with the Innovators but toned down somewhat. They are also attracted to new technologies and practices, primarily because they are trying to get a big "win" before anyone else does. Early adopters don't fail as often as innovators, so they are respected opinion leaders in their organizations. They are role models for other adopters.

Innovators and Early Adopters have a few attributes in common. They are both attracted to innovation for its own sake. They are looking for revolutionary, game-changing gains. They are highly risk-tolerant and highly motivated to see the change work. They are willing to exert substantial personal energy and initiative to make the change work. They will read, seek out colleagues, experiment, and so on. They see challenges with the new thing as opportunities to make the new thing work before others do. Bottom line is that these people can succeed with little external support.

Now, the big question: Who typically works on pilot teams?

Innovators and Early Adopters! This is problematic because Innovators and Early Adopters are not representative of the majority of adopters in the organization, and they represent a fairly small percentage of adopters in the organization.

As Figure 22-3 shows, the innovation adoption sequence is a bell curve (a standard normal distribution). Innovators are the third standard deviation from the mean, and early adopters are the second. They represent 15% of the total adopters.

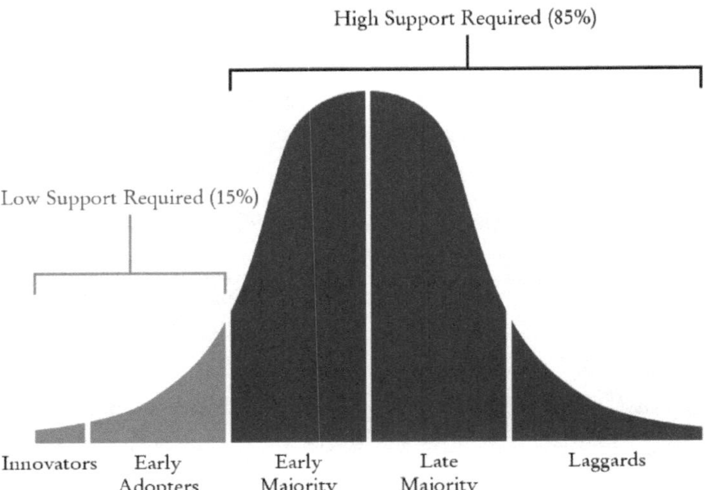

Figure 22-3

Different levels of support are required for different parts of the innovation adoption sequence. Later adopters require a higher level of support than earlier adopters.

In contrast with the earlier adopters, the later adopters (the last 85%) also have some characteristics in common. They are attracted to novelty for the sake of improved quality or productivity but not for the sake of innovation or novelty. They are looking for low-risk, safe, incremental gains. They are not very risk-tolerant, and many are risk-averse or highly risk-averse. Far from being willing to exert personal energy to overcome obstacles, the later adopters view obstacles as evidence that the change is a bad idea and should be abandoned. This group is not highly motivated to see the change succeed; their motivation ranges from being moderately motivated to see the change succeed to being moderately motivated to see the change fail.

What this means is that pilot teams don't tend to tell you most of what you need to know to lead a successful rollout.

Later adopters need more support, and most adopters are later adopters.

Some leaders in tech organizations will argue that their staffs consist of higher percentages of Innovators and Early Adopters and lower percentages of Late Majority and Laggards. Indeed, percentages can vary for different populations. However, it's more effective to assume a higher level of support is needed and scale that back if your adoption is progressing better than planned than it is to backfill support after your adoption has already stalled.

20,000-Foot Rollout View, Take 2

Here's the 20,000-foot view of a more reality-based Agile adoption approach.

Phase 1: Begin with a pilot team. Charter an initial team to trial an approach to Agile development in your organization. Work out the stumbling blocks at the single-team level.

Phase 2: Propagate Agile practices to one or more additional teams. Communicate a detailed vision of how Agile will benefit your organization and the people in it. Describe the benefits realized by the pilot team in detail. Communicate a detailed vision of how the Agile adoption will benefit the specific people on the next teams. Provide explicit training during work hours, coaching, and time to work on the rollout to the new teams. Check in regularly with the new teams and offer to provide additional support. Work out additional kinks, including inter-team issues. Develop a plan for the level of training and support needed for the larger scale rollout.

Phase 3: Roll out Agile practices to the entire organization. Communicate a revised vision of how Agile will benefit your organization based on the first few teams' experience. Describe the benefits realized by those teams in detail, and explain what lessons have been learned that will help guarantee that additional teams will be successful. Listen to people's feedback, and revise the vision as needed. Communicate the revised vision, and acknowledge that it includes people's feedback.

Schedule meetings with each person who will be affected by the Agile adoption, and communicate a detailed vision of how the Agile adoption will benefit that person specifically. Prepare for each of these meetings by understanding the individual's specific case; do not treat the individual just as a generic member of a group.

Describe the specific plan for making Agile successful in your organization. Describe who is leading the adoption effort, what tasks will be needed to make the adoption successful, and the timeline for adoption.

Provide training and coaching during work hours. Emphasize that each team has permission to do the work needed to make the rollout successful. Check in regularly with the teams and provide additional support. Make staff available to help work out issues within teams and across teams. Explain that challenges are expected and support will be available when challenges occur.

Inspect and Adapt

As the rollout continues, refer back to the Lippitt/Knoster model periodically, looking for signs of problems in each area. Each adoption is unique in some respects. Be open to feedback and changing direction if needed. This is an opportunity to model Inspect and Adapt behavior at the leadership level.

Suggested Leadership Actions

Inspect

- Review the Lippitt/Knoster model and how it applies to your past or current change initiatives. In what parts of the model has your organization typically been successful, and where is there room for improvement?
- Reflect on the innovation diffusion model and how it applies to your organization's track record with pilot teams. Do you agree that your pilot teams have consisted of Innovators and Early Adopters? How representative have they been of the rest of your organization?

Adapt

- Based on a gap analysis between your current Agile adoption and the Lippitt/Knoster model's categories, create a plan to improve performance in the gaps.
- Based on the gap analysis between your current support for later Adopters and the innovation diffusion model, create a plan to provide a level of support appropriate for your later adopters.

Additional Resources

Here are two resources directly related to the issues discussed in this chapter.

Rogers, Everett M. 1995. *Diffusion of Innovation, 4th Ed.* New York : The Free Press, 1995. This is the definitive work on innovation diffusion.

Moore, Geoffrey. 1991. *Crossing the Chasm, Revised Ed.* New York, NY : Harper Business, 1991. This book popularized Rogers' work on innovation diffusion. It's highly readable and much shorter than Rogers' book.

Beyond the specific considerations in this chapter, organizational change is a huge topic, and there's a lot of general business literature that is worth reading. Here are two of the best books I've found:

Maxwell, John C. 2007. *The 21 Irrefutable Laws of Leadership.* Nashville, Tennessee: Thomas Nelson, 2007. Maxwell's book is a good counterpoint to the sometimes-overly-analytical approach to leadership that I see from software leaders. He includes key advice, such as "the heart comes before the head" and "People don't care how much you know until they know how much you care."

Heifetz, Ronald A. and Marty Linsky. 2017. *Leadership on the Line: Staying Alive Through the Dangers of Change, Revised Ed.* Boston, Massachusetts : Harvard Business Review Press, 2017. This is a somewhat dry book that nonetheless provides a really useful way to think about the leader's role in leading change ("view from the balcony") and some important and seldom-discussed obstacles to change.

6699 CLOSING

6700

6701

6702

Enjoy the Fruits of Your Labor

From the beginning, “Agile” has served both as a rallying cry for better software development practices and as an umbrella term for a large collection of practices, principles, and philosophies that have been developed in support of that rallying cry.

Organizations’ implementations of Agile practices vary tremendously—some organizations commit to becoming more responsive to change from top to bottom, while others focus on improving productivity and quality at the individual team level.

What these organizations have in common is the skilled use of carefully selected practices that have been proven to work—including both traditional practices and modern Agile practices.

When this is done well, the organization creates teams that understand the capabilities of the practices they are using and that use the practices effectively.

The teams stay focused on the goals of the organization. The teams are responsive to the organization's needs, even when they change, which supports the organization by responding to its customers' changing needs.

The teams continuously monitor their workflows. They know where the work is and whether it's progressing as it should, and they provide extensive visibility to others. They deliver what they say they are going to deliver, when they say they are going to deliver it, with high quality.

Surprises are few and far between. In the event of unpleasant surprises, the teams provide early notification, which allows both the teams and the rest of the organization to respond quickly and effectively.

The teams work well together, with other teams, with other project stakeholders, and with the world beyond their organization.

The teams maintain high quality at all times and identify opportunities for improvement regularly. Motivation is high and attrition is low.

As an organization progresses toward this vision of effective software development, it will move through a few maturation phases.

Initially, the focus will be on team performance. Teams will require several sprints to learn Scrum and other supporting Agile practices. They will work on their ability to plan in small increments, design in ways that support short iterations, prioritize, commit, maintain high quality, make decisions on behalf of their organization, work together as a team, and deliver.

Over time, the focus will shift to project-level decisions. The teams' capacity will increase, and the organization will need to support the teams with good project leadership, clear product leadership on requirements and other priorities, and timely decision making to leverage the team's proven increased capacity.

Eventually, the focus will shift to organizational decisions. The teams will be able to deliver quickly and change direction quickly. This opens up opportunities for the organization to plan and execute differently and better, using its enhanced development capability.

The focus on a growth mindset and on inspect and adapt means that, over time, all of this just gets better and better. Enjoy!

Summary of Key Principles

Inspect and Adapt. Agile is an empirical approach that depends on learning from experience. This requires creating opportunities to reflect periodically and make adjustments based on experience.

Start with Scrum. Scrum is not necessarily the final destination on an Agile journey, but it is the most-structured, best-supported place to start.

Build Cross-Functional Teams. Work on Agile projects occurs within self-managed teams. To be self-managed, teams must include the full set of skills needed to make well-informed decisions that are binding on the organization.

Motivate Teams Through Autonomy, Mastery, and Purpose. Agile practices inherently support the factors that contribute to motivation. Teams are intended to work autonomously, to become better over time (mastery), and in order to work autonomously they need to understand their purpose. The concepts of "healthy Agile team" and "motivated Agile team" are strongly intertwined.

Keep Projects Small. Small projects are easier and more often successful. Not all work can be structured into small projects, but the work that can be structured that way should be.

Keep Sprints Short. Short sprints support a frequent Inspect and Adapt feedback loop. They expose problems quickly, making it easy to nip small problems in the bud before they become large problems.

Use Velocity-Based Planning. Plans are made based on experience, which is an instance of Agile's empirical focus.

Deliver in Vertical Slices. Feedback is important in Agile, and teams get better feedback both from customers and on their technology and design choices when they deliver in vertical slices rather than horizontal slices.

Develop a Growth Mindset. Whether you look at it from the point of view of the Mastery part of Autonomy, Mastery, and Purpose or from the point of view of Inspect and Adapt, effective Agile teams maintain a steady focus on getting better.

Develop Business Focus. A good understanding of the business can make up for a lot of sins in other areas. Developers frequently have to fill in gaps in requirements and in conversations with their Product Owner. Understanding their business helps them fill those gaps in ways that will be beneficial to the business.

Minimize the Defect Detection Gap. The cost to fix a defect tends to grow the longer it stays in process. A benefit of Agile's focus on continuous quality work is detecting more defects closer to the source.

Create and Use a Definition of Done. A good Definition of Done helps minimize the gap between defect insertion and detection.

Maintain a Potentially Releasable Level of Quality. Maintaining a potentially releasable level of quality helps to catch additional defects that slip through an earlier DoD.

Refine the Product Backlog. Keep the team well-fed with high-quality requirements.

Integrate Testers into the Development Teams. Tighten the feedback loop between development and test by having the people doing the work work more closely together.

Use Automated Tests, Created by the Development Team. Automated tests help to minimize the defect detection gap.

Automate Repetitive Activities. No one likes repetitive activities, and many of the activities that can be automated in software development provide more benefit when they're automated than when they aren't.

Manage to Outcomes, Not Details. Support your team's autonomy.

Express Clear Purpose with Commander's Intent. Support your teams' autonomy *and purpose.*

Prioritize, and Communicate Priorities. Provide your teams with the guidance they need to make decisions that align with your organizational objectives.

Focus on Throughput, Not Activity. A variation of managing to outcomes, but adding the nuance that busy-ness is not the objective—getting valuable work done is the objective.

Model Key Agile Behaviors. Effective leaders model the behaviors they want to see in others.

Decriminalize Mistakes. You can't have a growth mentality or make meaningful use of Inspect and Adapt if your teams get in trouble when they admit they did something wrong. Decriminalize mistakes so that they're made visible without hesitation and you can learn from them. A mistake you don't learn from penalizes your organization twice.

Support Large Agile Projects Through Architecture. Good architecture can support portioned work on a project and minimize large-project overhead. Great architecture can make a large project feel like a small one.

Tighten Feedback Loops. Don't take any longer to learn lessons than you need to; keep the feedback loops as tight as possible. This supports more rapid progress from Inspect and Adapt and faster improvements in effectiveness from a growth mindset.

Fix the System, Not the Individual. Most software professionals want to do good work. If they aren't doing good work, and especially if it seems like they're trying not to do good work, be sure you understand the dynamics that are contributing to that. Don't blame the person—look for the problem in the system that's probably frustrating the person. Fix the system instead of the person, and give yourself a more motivated, higher morale employee.

Bibliography

AAMI. 2012. *Guidance on the use of AGILE practices in the development of medical device software.* 2012. AAMI TIR45 2012.

Adzic, Gojko and David Evans. 2014. *Fifty Quick Ideas to Improve Your User Stories.* s.l. : Neuri Consulting LLP, 2014.

Aghina, Wouter, et al. 2019. *How to select and develop individuals for successful agile teams: A practical guide.* s.l. : McKinsey & Company, 2019.

Alignment at Scale. **Kniberg, Henrik. 2016.** Johannesburg, South Africa : s.n., 2016. Agile Africa.

Bass, Len, et al. 2012. *Software Architecture in Practice, 3rd Ed.* s.l. : Addison-Wesley Professional, 2012.

Beck, Kent and Cyanthia Andres. 2005. *Extreme Programm Explained: Embrace Change, 2nd Ed.* Boston : Addison-Wesley, 2005.

Beck, Kent. 2000. *Extreme Programming Explained: Embrace Change.* Reading, Massachusetts : Addison-Wesley, 2000.

Bernstein, David. 2015. *Beyond Legacy Code: Nine Practices to Extend the Life (and Value) of Your Software.* Dallas, Texas : The Pragmatic Bookshelf, 2015.

Boehm, Barry and Richard Turner. 2004. *Balancing Agility and Discipline: A Guide for the Perplexed.* Boston : Addison-Wesley, 2004.

Boehm, Barry. 1981. *Software Engineering Economics.* Englewood Cliffs, New Jersey : Prentice-Hall, 1981.

Boehm, Barry W. 1988. A Spiral Model of Software Development and Enhancement. May 1988.

Boehm, Barry, et al. 2000. *Software Cost Estimation with Cocomo II.* Upper Saddle River, New Jersey : Prentice Hall PTR, 2000.

Boyd, John R. 2007. *Patterns of Conflict.* January 2007.

Brooks, Fred. 1975. *Mythical Man-Month.* Reading, Massachusetts : Addison-Wesley, 1975.

Building and Scaling High Performing Technology Organizations. **Humble, Jez. October 26, 2018.** Seattle, WA : s.n., October 26, 2018. Construx Software Leadership Summit.

Carnegie, Dale. 1936. *How to Win Friends and Influence People.* New York : Simon & Schuster, 1936.

Cherniss, Cary, Ph.D. 1999. The business case for emotional intelligence. [Online] 1999. [Cited: January 25, 2019.] https://emedia.rmit.edu.au/leadrmit/sites/default/files/The%20Business%20Case%20for%20Emotional%20Intelligence.pdf.

Cohn, Mike. 2010. *Succeeding with Agile: Software Development Using Scrum.* Upper Saddle River, New Jersey : Addison-Wesley, 2010.

—. 2004. *User Stories Applied: For Agile Software Development.* s.l. : Addison-Wesley, 2004.

Collyer, Keith and Jordi Manzano. 2013. Being agile while still being compliant: A practical approach for medical device manufacturers. [Online] March 5, 2013. [Cited: January 20, 2019.] https://www.ibm.com/developerworks/rational/library/compliant-agile-medical-device/compliant-agile-medical-device-pdf.pdf.

Conway, Melvin E. 1968. How do Committees Invent? *Datamation.* April 1968.

Coram, Robert. 2002. *Boyd: The Fighter Pilot Who Changed the Art of War.* New York : Back Bay Books, 2002.

Crispin, Lisa and Janet Gregory. 2009. *Agile Testing: A Practical Guide for Testers and Agile Teams.* s.l. : Addison-Wesley Professional, 2009.

Cusumano, Michael A. and Richard Selby. 1995. *Microsoft Secrets: How the World's Most Powerful Software Company Creates Technology, Shapes Markets and Manages People.* New York, NY : Touchstone, 1995.

DeMarco, Tom. 2002. *Slack: Getting Past Burnout, Busywork, and the Myth of Total Efficiency.* s.l. : Broadway Books, 2002.

Derby, Esther and Diana Larsen. 2006. *Agile Retrospectives: Making Good Teams Great.* s.l. : Pragmatic Bookshelf, 2006.

DORA. 2018. *2018 Accelerate: State of Devops.* s.l. : DevOps Research and Assessment, 2018.

Doyle, Michael and David Strauss. 1993. *How to Make Meetings Work!* New York : Jove Books, 1993.

DZone Research. 2015. *The Guide to Continuous Delivery.* s.l. : Sauce Labs, 2015.

Feathers, Michael. 2004. *Working Effectively with Legacy Code.* Upper Saddle River, New Jersey : Prentice Hall PTR, 2004.

Fisher, Roger and William Ury. 2011. *Getting to Yes: Negotiating Agreement Without Giving In, 3rd Ed.* New York : Penguin Books, 2011.

Forsgren, Nicole, et al. 2018. *Accelerate: The Science of Lean Software and DevOps: Building and Scaling High Performing Technology Organizations.* Portland, OR : IT Revolution, 2018.

Gilb, Tom. 1988. *Principles of Software Engineering Management.* Wokingham, England : Addison-Wesley, 1988.

Goleman, Daniel. 2004. What Makes a Leader? *Harvard Business Review.* January 2004.

Gould, Stephen Jay. 1977. *Ever Since Darwin.* s.l. : WW Norton & Co Inc, 1977.

Grenning, James. 2001. Launching Extreme Programming at a Process-Intensive Company. *IEEE Software.* November/December 2001.

Hammarberg, Marcus and Joakim Sunden. 2014. *Kanban in Action.* Shelter Island, NY : Manning Publications, 2014.

Heifetz, Ronald A. and Marty Linsky. 2017. *Leadership on the Line: Staying Alive Through the Dangers of Change, Revised Ed.* Boston, Massachusetts : Harvard Business Review Press, 2017.

Humble, Jez, et al. 2015. *Lean Enterprise: How High Performance Organizations Innovate at Scale.* Sebastopol, CA : O'Reilly Media, 2015.

James, Geoffrey. 2018. It's Official: Open-Plan Offices Are Now the Dumbest Management Fad of All Time. *Inc.* July 16, 2018.

Jarrett, Christian. 2018. Open-plan offices drive down face-to-face interactions and increase use of email. *BPS Research.* July 5, 2018.

—. 2013. The supposed benefits of open-plan offices do not outweigh the costs. *BPS Research.* August 19, 2013.

Jones, Capers and Olivier Bonsignour. 2012. *The Economics of Software Quality.* Upper Saddle River, New Jersey : Addison-Wesley, 2012.

Jones, Capers. 1991. *Applied Software Measurement: Assuring Productivity and Quality.* New York : McGraw-Hill, 1991.

Kim, Gene, et al. 2016. *The DevOps Handbook.* Portland, Oregon : IT Revolution Press, 2016.

Konnikova, Maria. 2014. The Open-Office Trap. *New Yorker.* January 7, 2014.

Lacey, Mitch. 2016. *The Scrum Field Guide: Agile Advice for Your First Year and Beyond, 2d Ed.* Upper Saddle River, NJ : Addison-Wesley, 2016.

Leffingwell, Dean. 2011. *Agile Software Requirements: Lean Requirements Practices for Teams, Programs, and the Enterprise.* Boston, Massachusetts : Pearson Education, Inc., 2011.

Lencioni, Patrick. 2002. *The Five Dysfunctions of a Team.* San Francisco, California : Jossey-Bass, 2002.

Martin, Robert C. 2017. *Clean Architecture: A Craftsman's Guide to Software Structure and Design.* s.l. : Prentice Hall, 2017.

Maxwell, John C. 2007. *The 21 Irrefutable Laws of Leadership.* Nashville, Tennessee : Thomas Nelson, 2007.

McConnell, Steve and Jenny Stuart. 2018. Agile Technical Coach Career Path. [Online] 2018. https://www.construx.com/whitepapers.

—. 2018. Career Pathing for Software Professionals. [Online] 2018. https://www.construx.com/whitepapers.

—. 2018. Software Architect Career Path. [Online] 2018. https://www.construx.com/whitepapers.

—. 2018. Software Product Owner Career Path. [Online] 2018. https://www.construx.com/whitepapers.

—. 2018. Software Quality Manager Career Path. [Online] 2018. https://www.construx.com/whitepapers.

—. 2018. Software Technical Manager Career Path. [Online] 2018. https://www.construx.com/whitepapers.

McConnell, Steve. 2004. *Code Complete, 2nd Ed.* Redmond, Washington : Microsoft Press, 2004.

—. 2016. Measuring Software Development Productivity. [Online] 2016. [Cited: January 19, 2019.] https://resources.construx.com/construx-webinars/measuring-software-development-productivity-webinar/.

—. 2004. *Professional Software Development.* Boston, Massachusetts : Addison-Wesley, 2004.

—. 1996. *Rapid Development: Taming Wild Software Schedules.* Redmond, Washington : Microsoft Press, 1996.

—. 2000. Sitting on the Suitcase. *IEEE Software.* May/June 2000.

—. 2006. *Software Estimation: Demystifying the Black Art.* Redmond, Washington : Microsoft Press, 2006.

—. 2006. *Software Estimation: Demystifying the Black Art.* Redmond, Washington : Microsoft Press, 2006.

—. 2019. Understanding Software Projects Lecture Series. *Construx OnDemand.* [Online] 2019. https://ondemand.construx.com.

—. 2011. What does 10x mean? Measuring Variations in Programmer Productivity. [book auth.] Andy and Greg Wilson, Eds Oram. *Making Software: What Really Works, and Why We Believe It.* Sebastopol, CA : O'Reilly, 2011.

Moore, Dave. 1996. Private Communication. 1996.

Moore, Geoffrey. 1991. *Crossing the Chasm, Revised Ed.* New York, NY : Harper Business, 1991.

Mulqueen, Casey and David Collins. 2014. *Social Style & Versatility Facilitator Handbook.* Centennial, Colorado : TRACOM Press, 2014.

Nygard, Michael T. 2018. *Release It!: Design and Deploy Production-Ready Software, 2nd Ed.* s.l. : Pragmatic Bookshelf, 2018.

Oosterwal, Dantar P. 2010. *The Lean Machine: How Harley-Davidson Drove Top-Line Growth and Profitability with Revolutionary Lean Product Development.* New York, NY : AMACOM, 2010.

Patterson, Kerry, et al. 2002. *Crucial Conversations: Tools for talking when the stakes are high.* New York : McGraw-Hill, 2002.

Patton, Jeff. 2014. *User Story Mapping: Discover the Whole Story, Build the Right Product.* s.l. : O'Reilly Media, 2014.

Pink, Daniel H. 2009. *Drive: The Surprising Truth About What Motivates Us.* New York : Riverhead Books, 2009.

Poole, Charles and Jan Willem Huisman. 2001. Using Extreme Programming in a Maintenance Environment. *IEEE Software.* November/December 2001.

Poppendieck, Mary and Tom. 2006. *Implementing Lean Software Development.* s.l. : Addison-Wesley Professional, 2006.

Puppet Labs. 2014. *2014 State of DevOps Report.* 2014.

Putnam, Lawrence H., and and Ware Myers. 1992. *Measures for Excellence: Reliable Software On Time, Within Budget.* Englewood Cliffs, New Jersey : Yourdon Press, 1992.

Reinertsen, Donald G. 2009. *The Principles of Product Development Flow: Second Generation Lean Product Development.* Redondo Beach, California : Celeritas Publishing, 2009.

Richards, Chet. 2004. *Certain to Win: The Strategy of John Boyd, Applied to Business.* s.l. : Xlibris Corporation, 2004.

Robertson, Robertson Suzanne and James. 2013. *Mastering the Requirements Process: Getting Requirements Right, 3rd Ed.* Upper Saddle River, New Jersey : Addison-Wesley, 2013.

Rogers, Everett M. 1995. *Diffusion of Innovation, 4th Ed.* New York : The Free Press, 1995.

Rother, Mike. 2010. *Toyota Kata: Managing People for Improvement, Adaptiveness and Superior Results.* s.l. : McGraw-Hill, 2010.

Rozovsky, Julia. 2015. The five keys to a successful Google team. [Online] November 17, 2015. [Cited: November 25, 2018.] https://rework.withgoogle.com/blog/five-keys-to-a-successful-google-team/.

Rubin, Kenneth. 2012. *Essential Scrum: A Practical Guide to the Most Popular Agile Process.* s.l. : Addison-Wesley, 2012.

Schuh, Peter. 2001. Recovery, Redemption, and Extreme Programming. *IEEE Software.* November/December 2001.

Schwaber, Ken and Jeff Sutherland. 2017. *The Scrum Guide: The Definitive Guide to Scrum: The Rules of the Game.* 2017.

Scrum Alliance. 2017. *State of Scrum 2017-2018.* 2017.

Sharma, Sanjeev and Bernie Coyne. *DevOps for Dummies.* Hoboken, New Jersey : John Wiley & Sons.

Snowden, David J. and Mary E. Boone. 2007. A Leader's Framework for Decision Making. *Harvard Business Review.* November 2007.

Standish Group. 2013. *Chaos Manifesto 2013: Think Big, Act Small.* 2013.

Stellman, Andrew and Jennifer Green. 2013. *Learning Agile: Understanding Scrum, XP, Lean, and Kanban.* s.l. : O'Reilly Media, 2013.

Stuart, Jenny and Melvin Perez. 2018. Retrofitting Legacy Systems with Unit Tests. [Online] July 2018. https://www.construx.com/whitepapers.

Stuart, Jenny, et al. 2018. Six Things Every Software Executive Should Know About Scrum. [Online] 2018. https://www.construx.com/whitepapers.

—. 2017. Staffing Scrum Roles. [Online] 2017. https://www.construx.com/whitepapers.

—. 2018. Succeeding with Geographically Distributed Scrum. [Online] 2018. https://www.construx.com/whitepapers.

—. 2018. Ten Keys to Successful Scrum Adoption. [Online] 2018. https://www.construx.com/whitepapers.

—. 2018. Ten Pitfalls of Enterprise Agile Adoption. [Online] 2018. https://www.construx.com/whitepapers.

Sutherland, Jeff. 2014. *Scrum: The Art of Doing Twice the Work in Half the Time.* New York : Crown Business, 2014.

The Four Way Test. About the Four Way Test. *The Four Way Test.* [Online] [Cited: January 12, 2019.] http://thefourwaytest.com/history-of-the-four-way-test/.

Tockey, Steve. 2005. *Return on Software: Maximizing the Return on Your Software Investment.* Boston : Addison-Wesley, 2005.

Twardochleb, Michal. 2017. Optimal selection of team members according to Belbin's theory. *Scientific Journals of the Maritime University of Szczecin.* September 15, 2017.

U.S. Marine Corps Staff. 1989. *Warfighting: The U.S. Marine Corp Book of Strategy.* New York : Currency Doubleday, 1989.

Velocity Culture (The Unmet Challenge in Ops). **Jenkins, Jon. June 16, 2011.** June 16, 2011. O'Reilly Velocity Conference.

Westrum, Ron. 2005. A Typology of Organisational Cultures. January 2005, pp. 22-27.

Wiegers, Karl and Joy Beatty. 2013. *Software Requirements, 3rd Ed.* Redmond, Washington : Microsoft Press, 2013.

Wikipedia. 2018. OODA Loop. *Wikipedia.* [Online] November 28, 2018. [Cited: November 28, 2018.] https://en.wikipedia.org/wiki/OODA_loop.

Williams, Laurie and Robert Kessler. 2002. *Pair Programming Illuminated.* Boston, Mass. : Addison-Wesley, 2002.

Wynne, Matt, et al. 2017. *The Cucumber Book: Behaviour-Driven Development for Testers and Developers, 2nd Ed.* s.l. : Pragmatic Programmers, 2017.

Yale Center for Emotional Intelligence. The RULER Model. [Online] [Cited: January 19, 2019.]

❧ ☙

Acknowledgments

Thanks first and foremost to my technical colleagues at Construx Software. I have the good fortune to work with a remarkably intelligent, talented, and experienced staff, and this book—largely a summary of our collective experiences over the past 20 years—would not be possible without their contributions. Thanks to **Jenny Stuart**, VP of Consulting, for her incredible experience and insights working on large-scale Agile adoptions. I appreciate her comments on navigating organizational issues in large organizations. Thanks to **Matt Peloquin**, CTO, for his expertise, unrivaled worldwide after leading more than 500 architecture reviews, in software architecture and the role it plays in Agile implementations. Thanks to **Earl Beede**, Senior Fellow, consultant and instructor extraordinaire, for his insights into the clearest ways of presenting Agile concepts so that the audience understands them and can implement them effectively. Thanks to **Melvin Pérez-Cedano**, Senior Fellow, for his combination of worldwide experience and capacious book knowledge. Thank you, Melvin, for being my walking reference resource for this project and a key guide to the practices that work most effectively. Thanks to **Erik Simmons**, Senior Fellow, for being a bottomless well of knowledge about research in uncertainty and complexity and for his expert guidance in implementing Agile practices in large-scale, traditional companies. Thanks to **Steve Tockey**, Principle Consultant, for his deep insight and unmatched foundational knowledge about traditional, rigorous software practices and how they interplay with Agile practices. Thank you, Steve, for always making sure I remember that Agile is a set of practices, not a religion. Thanks to **Bob Webber**, Senior Fellow, for his insights into Agile product management—his decades of leadership experience have helped focus this book on what leaders need. And, finally, thanks to **John Clifford**, Agile Practices Lead, for his track record of encouraging, coaching, exhorting, and occasionally compelling organizations to realize all the value they should from their Agile adoptions. What an incredible group! I have been so fortunate to work with these people.

Other acknowledgments tbd …

Index

TBD

❧ ☙

About the Author

STEVE MCCONNELL is best-known as the author of *Code Complete*, a software industry classic that is often described as the best-reviewed, best-selling software development book of all time. Steve's books have been translated into more than 20 languages and sold more than one million copies worldwide.

Steve's company, Construx Software, has been helping software organizations improve their capabilities for more than 20 years. Construx's vision is *to make every software project successful by advancing the professional effectiveness of individuals, teams, and organizations.*

For more information, see www.stevemcconnell.com or email Steve at stevemcc@construx.com.

How much would your teams benefit from being

CODE Complete

"Steve McConnell is one of those rare souls who practice the state of the art and demystify it too"
– John Vlissides, Co-author, *Design Patterns*

Widely considered one of the best practical guides to programming, Steve McConnell's *Code Complete* has been helping developers write better code for more than a decade. This book includes hundreds of code samples that illustrate the art and science of software construction. Capturing the body of knowledge available from research, academia, and everyday commercial practice, McConnell synthesizes the most effective techniques and know-how principles into clear, pragmatic guidance. No matter what your experience level, development environment, or project size, this book will inform and stimulate your thinking—and help you build the highest quality code.

"An excellent guide to programming style and software construction."
– Martin Fowler, *Refactoring*

"What you need to know to be a professional developer."
– Kent Beck, *Extreme Programming Explained*

Order copies for your team today!

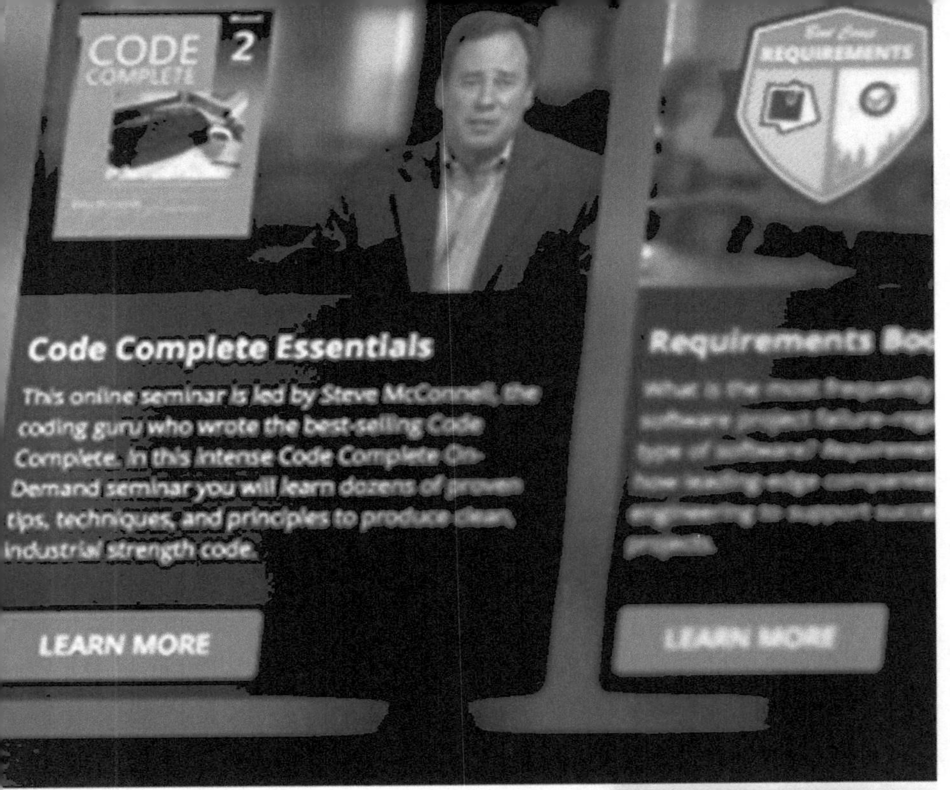

Steve McConnell On Demand

See Steve's lectures on *Code Complete* and *Understanding Software Projects* on the Construx OnDemand website at **ondemand.construx.com**.

For discounts on Steve's lectures visit the *More Effective Agile* website at **MoreEffectiveAgile.com**.